NEGOTIATE IT!

*How to Crush Your Fears,
Develop Your Negotiation Muscle,
and Gain Power in the Workplace*

NEGOTIATE IT!

*How to Crush Your Fears,
Develop Your Negotiation Muscle,
and Gain Power in the Workplace*

E. LYNN PRICE

Disclaimer:

The content of this book is for informational purposes only and not for the purpose of providing legal advice. You should contact your attorney to obtain advice with respect to any particular issue or problem. Use of this book does not create an attorney-client relationship.

All rights reserved. No part of this publication may be reproduced, distributed, or transmitted in any form or by any means, including photocopying, recording, or other electronic or mechanical methods, without the prior written permission of the publisher, except in the case of brief quotations embodied in reviews and certain other non-commercial uses permitted by copyright law.

ISBN: 0-692-15253-9
ISBN-13: 978-0-692-15253-9
Copyright © 2018, Lynn Price Consulting, LLC
Publishing Services by Happy Self Publishing
www.happyselfpublishing.com

First Edition 2018

DEDICATION

To My Dad.

The first person to teach me the concept of "Don't Ask, Don't Get."

Thank you for both challenging and encouraging me to aim high, treat people well and do the hard work. And to keep a sense of humor along the way (by far, the best part!).

You're a good dad, Dad!

TABLE OF CONTENTS

ACKNOWLEDGMENTS ix

INTRODUCTION 1

SECTION I WHY NEGOTIATE AND
COMMON EXCUSES TO AVOID 5

SECTION II BE READY 35

SECTION III BE RELATABLE 77

SECTION IV BE REASONABLE 129

SECTION V ADDITIONAL TOOLS AND
STRATEGIES 163

SECTION VI GETTING STARTED 201

SECTION VII NOW IT'S YOUR TURN! 215

ABOUT THE AUTHOR 217

ACKNOWLEDGMENTS

My sincerest thanks to my husband for endless amounts of encouragement, support and laughter over the last 20+ years. And my son. For being proud of me for tackling such a big project and for asking "How's your book coming?" every week until it was done!

Thank you to all my family for providing encouragement, but also for being one of the funniest, best story-telling groups I've ever had the privilege to be around. If family is a lottery, I hit the jackpot.

My heartfelt thanks to my good friends Jen, Maggie, Gayle, Kathryn, Patrick, and all my amazing Centurion friends, especially Jim Allin. Jim's creative selection of "reverse incentives" was instrumental in getting me to complete this book. Sorry, "Tiger Scholarship Fund," no money for you this year! And special thanks to Lise Cartwright for her valuable advice and guidance.

> "AMONG THOSE WHOM I LIKE OR ADMIRE, I CAN FIND NO COMMON DENOMINATOR, BUT AMONG THOSE WHOM I LOVE, I CAN: ALL OF THEM MAKE ME LAUGH."
> – W.H. AUDEN, POET.

10% of the profits of "Negotiate It!" will be donated to "Harvesters: The Community Food Network," a Charity Navigator 4-star ranked food bank.

How to Use this Book

1. If you want to learn *why* you should dedicate time to improving your negotiation muscle and how to address the fear and four common misconceptions associated with the process, start at the beginning.

2. If you want to jump in and learn the strategy behind The Three R's Formula, start with the "Be Ready" chapter.

3. If you don't like personal stories, skip all of the "Real Life Example" insets.

4. If you want infographics on how to a) overcome your fear of negotiation, b) get an overview of The Three R's Formula for negotiation, or c) get a pre-negotiation checklist, go to www.negotiateitbook.com for a free download.

And if you think that this book would help a friend or colleague, please consider giving them a copy as a gift!

Note: Names of some people in this book have been changed to respect their privacy.

Visit www.lynnpriceconsulting.com to contact Lynn about doing personalized training on this and other topics.

INTRODUCTION

Negotiation can be intimidating. People often view this as a skill you either have or you don't. And if you think you "don't have it," you might even fear it. Fear that you will fail. Fear that you will embarrass yourself, your company, or others. Fear that you'll be seen as a fraud or imposter. You ask yourself, "Can I *really* be successful in getting what I want?" "Why would someone change their offer, terms, or price simply because I *ask* them to?" "What if they get mad at me for asking?"

But the real problem with negotiation isn't that it's difficult or that only a gifted few can do it well. Instead, the real issue is that you haven't been taught an easy, applicable way to negotiate. And you haven't practiced in low-risk circumstances where you can build your negotiation muscles!

If you are fearful and don't know where to start, you can easily fall into the "Don't Ask, Don't Get" trap. Because if you never ask, you'll never get what you want or need.

I've created a simple formula that helps you improve your negotiations immediately. This method focuses on The Three R's Formula. You need to be:

- Ready
- Relatable
- Reasonable

I've selected these three categories because, in my negotiation experience, these are the things that make people the *most* effective in the *least* amount of time. They are the "8 Minute Abs" of the negotiation world. But these tips actually work!

In this book, you will learn how to "Make the Ask."

You'll develop confidence in both defining and asking for what you want. You'll learn to defend your position, anticipate pushback, and complete your negotiation strategically and efficiently.

Who Am I?

I have over twenty years of professional negotiation experience. Most of it has been as a corporate attorney working with different industries – from national telecommunications firm, to a national engineering company, to a small mergers and acquisition firm. And much of that that experience, believe it or not, was coming from a negotiating position of perceived weakness, where some would argue that we had very little or no leverage.

I've negotiated well over eleven thousand agreements. From simple and complex contracts to mergers and acquisitions, vendor/subcontractor agreements, salaries, houses, cars, and even a few family pets! I've also trained over a dozen attorneys/paralegals as well as hundreds of professionals on how to negotiate in a confident and effective manner.

I've encountered all types of negotiation styles and personalities. Much like the classic Clint Eastwood movie, I've seen "The Good, the Bad, and the Ugly!" I've seen what works and what doesn't. I can show you the most effective path and easiest way to get "wins." This way, you'll see the tangible value of learning a new skill. Seeing positive results will encourage you to look for negotiation opportunities everywhere you go! And yes, you can negotiate for the best deal without being perceived as a jerk. You can be pleasant while being a powerful negotiator.

When you apply these principles, you'll be able to make more money, save more money, and get more opportunities for unique experiences. But most importantly, you will gain confidence. And this confidence can spill over to many areas of your life. Confidence is like an invisible superpower! When you have it, you feel it. And others do too.

WARNING!

Developing this skill, like anything worthwhile, will take practice. But don't worry — I'll show you exactly how to do it! But I need you to start now. Don't let fear stop you from gaining a valuable skill. This is an opportunity to learn and improve. Don't leave things on the table. You need to "Make the Ask" and start now. Don't wait.

If you adopt and apply these recommendations, you will get results! And as an added benefit this skill applies to *both* your professional and personal life. Trust me; you are already negotiating. If you think you don't negotiate now, think back over the past month. How many times did you talk to friends about where to go to dinner? What movie to see? Who was driving? This book will teach you how to become more knowledgeable and strategic. But remember: "Don't Ask, Don't Get." Trust me; you can do it!

Now let's get started.

SECTION I

WHY NEGOTIATE AND COMMON EXCUSES TO AVOID

> "FINDING WHY IS A PROCESS OF
> DISCOVERY, NOT INVENTION."
> – SIMON SINEK, AUTHOR.

The first thing you should ask when you're learning a new skill is simply why bother?

- Why should you spend time learning about negotiation?
- Why should you negotiate at all?

Defining your "why" is what keeps you motivated. It's the cornerstone which reminds you why your work and effort is necessary and worthwhile. Identifying *your* "why" means defining what drives *you*. It will help keep you on track so "shiny objects" don't distract you and pull you off course. A well-developed "why" should be much more than just "making money." But saving and making money certainly are nice by-products of being a good negotiator!

While I can't define your "why," I can explain why *I* choose to negotiate on a daily basis. There are two main reasons.

1. To get what I want and need. In order to get what you want out of a situation, you have to ask for it. No one is going to read your mind. You have to "Make the Ask." This is the concept of "Don't Ask, Don't Get," which I'll refer to often in this book.

If you can stand up for yourself in a variety of situations and ask for what you want, you are engaging in self-respectful behavior. And exercising self-respect not only increases your sense of value, but it raises your confidence level. Funny enough, when you have confidence, your negotiations improve. As I mentioned in the introduction, confidence is like an invisible superpower — you can feel it and so can those around you! This confidence can also manifest in your nonverbal communications and can create an air of positivity and strength.

Consider the following. You are in a meeting and two people enter the room. One walks in with shoulders sloped, head down making no eye contact, and quietly sinks into his chair. The second person walks in with her head high, shoulders back, and makes eye contact with multiple people while smiling. She takes the time to make introductions and says hello to those she knows. Then she welcomes people who enter the room. She makes people feel comfortable.

Who would you rather engage with? The "squirrel" with the darting eyes or the person exuding confidence and warmth? I know whom I'd rather sit next to, and I know whom I'd listen to more. Confidence, whether real or faked, brings a positive atmosphere which attracts people to you. And don't worry, if you don't feel confident, we'll discuss ways to "fake it till you feel it."

2. To get the most out of a situation. I get upset when I feel that I'm being taken advantage of, so it motivates me to ensure that I don't leave anything on the table. I was instilled with this motivation at an early age.

When I was six years old, my parents gave my brother and me a toy that required joint ownership (never a good idea, for the record!). My brother is six years older and had his own take on "joint ownership." He announced that the toy was "all mine and half yours." And the worst part? I fell for it! I still remember feeling embarrassed and ashamed when I realized I was hoodwinked as "all mine and half yours" is not really a thing. Honestly, I'm still a little annoyed!

Most of us work hard for our money, so when you prevent yourself from giving it away unnecessarily, that's a tangible benefit – money saved that you can put to other uses. But don't misunderstand. When I talk about getting the most out of the situation, I'm in no way suggesting that you destroy personal or business relationships in the process. You don't need to wring every last drop of value out of each transaction. We'll discuss later when it's okay to leave some things on the table. Specifically, when you should let the other side have a "win" to preserve the long-term relationship.

There are few times where you will want to negotiate so hard that you sacrifice the relationship. Remember: it's a small world, and it's only getting smaller. Burning bridges should be a strategy which is rarely, if ever, used. We'll discuss this concept in detail in the last section "Additional Tools and Strategies."

Negotiation Excuses & How to Avoid Them

With your "why" in place to motivate you, it is time to get rid of any excuses preventing you from negotiating.

When I discuss negotiation with people who are reluctant to learn the skill, it's common for them to go to a handful of excuses to avoid the topic. Here are the most common "knee-jerk" excuses to avoid negotiation, as well as the reality that negates them.

Knee-Jerk Excuses	Truth
It's too aggressive.	Aggressive negotiation is a choice. You can be successful, often more so, while being Ready, Relatable, and Reasonable.
It's rude to ask someone to change their terms.	Asking, not demanding, for something you want is not rude behavior.
I don't know enough about the product, service, etc. to negotiate a better deal.	This is a legitimate concern, but also an easy fix. Do your homework and eliminate this as an excuse.

I don't want to make someone mad.	When done in a relatable and reasonable manner, 95% of people will not take offense to you "Making the Ask."
I would need formal training or a degree to negotiate successfully.	Nope. Practice is better than a pedigree when it comes to negotiation.
For females, it's considered "unfeminine" and aggressive. Ladies don't negotiate.	No. Just no. And because negotiation is really about communication, I argue that women can sometimes be *more* successful because they are natural communicators.

Identifying the Cause of Your Personal Obstacles

Even if you get rid of the excuses, there could still be subconscious obstacles standing in your way. Reviewing your negotiation history can help you identify and overcome any obstacles you've inadvertently created. By identifying the issue, naming it, and moving forward, you can turn any negative into a positive.

So what is your history with negotiation? Was it positive or negative? Perhaps you asked for something and got shot down harshly. Or someone made a big deal that what you were asking for was ridiculous. Because putting yourself "out there" by negotiating can be personal and intimidating at times, it only takes one or two negative interactions on this topic to turn people off.

When I was young, my mom took me to a craft fair. If history were any indicator, I'm sure I was getting on her nerves. So to buy herself some silence, literally, she gave me five dollars and told me I could buy something. I walked around all the craft booths carefully, clutching the five-dollar bill in my hands. This was the first time I had been given paper money for a transaction, so I felt excited and nervous.

I saw a few things I wanted to buy, but sadly, they were all less than five dollars. And even sadder . . . I didn't realize that you could spend *less* and get change back! I thought that because I had a five-dollar bill, I had to pay *exactly* five dollars. No one had told me otherwise.

So, I ended up buying a crocheted toilet paper "cozy" with a little boy sitting atop with a fishing pole. After all, who doesn't need a crocheted cozy to expertly camouflage toilet paper rolls in the bathroom? Ok, I really didn't want this eyesore, but I felt like I had to buy *something* and this was the best thing I could find for exactly five dollars.

When I returned to my mom, she burst out laughing. She asked why I would choose something so ugly. I explained that it was the only item that I found that cost exactly five dollars. That's when she told me that I could have spent less and introduced the concept of "change." A little late, I might add!

I was embarrassed and felt as if I failed my first adult mission with money. Consequently, I spent years feeling intimidated by financial transactions. I worried that I would make a huge mistake and embarrass myself again. Small things can sometimes have long-term consequences.

The point? Sometimes we allow one negative interaction to subconsciously define our relationship with a topic. I never *chose* to be afraid of money after "the toilet paper cozy incident." It just happened. And it wasn't until years later, while I was reading a book about financial literacy that I realized this connection and could correct it.

Common Negotiating Obstacles

The Worst Four-Letter Word – FEAR

> **"I'VE HAD A LOT OF WORRIES IN MY LIFE, MOST OF WHICH HAVE NEVER HAPPENED."**
> **- MARK TWAIN, WRITER/HUMORIST.**

The most common obstacle for someone initiating a negotiation is fear. Fear that we will make someone mad. Fear of rejection. Fear of failure.

Fortunately (and unfortunately), the only way to end negotiation fears is to jump in and do it. Once you have several negotiations under your belt, you will feel more confident and less fearful. Why? You either a) realized your fear was misplaced, blown out of proportion and it "wasn't as bad as you thought" or b) it went poorly and you learned from the experience. It's all about having a learner's mindset and being vulnerable enough to start practicing.

To be clear, bad negotiations will happen. They happen to beginners and experts alike. But, as long as you are willing to examine what went wrong, they can be beneficial in your learning curve. Don't let fear of negotiation make you miss an opportunity to improve and grow!

There are some truths you should know when you think about fear of negotiating. First, it's natural. Everyone experiences it at some level. And I mean everyone. It's not going away, so the only thing you can do is learn to manage your fear. The simple act of *acknowledging* fear is the first step in lessening its grip. Have you felt yourself become tense, nervous, and filled with anxiety? It can go on for a while until you recognize your feelings and then start to question what is creating such a response.

So it's important to identify your physical and mental fear manifestations. Do your shoulders tense up? Do you grind your teeth? Do you have a negative soundtrack running in your head: "You can't do this" or "You shouldn't be here"?

Once you realize the cause of your fear, for example, "I'm nervous calling this person, because they might be mad I'm asking for changes," you can troubleshoot your response and manage your reactions. In this scenario, when you realize their potential reaction is fueling your fear, you can address the specifics. "Okay, I'm prepared and I've thought of their potential responses. I have several responses ready, and if I get stumped, I'll handle it."

Once you identify the problem, you can start figuring out solutions, which will make you feel more in control. And the more control you feel, the less room there is for fear. And here is the best news about fear: when you name it and address it, your fear lessens. Awareness of your fear actually helps you detach from it. You begin to feel more confident. Fear may never go away, but it becomes manageable.

Quick fixes to address fear before or during a negotiation:

1. Over-prepare. Write note cards, use sticky notes, checklists, etc. Have things written down and prepare yourself with all the information you need to make your points.
2. Practice. Do dry runs with a partner. It's important to not run through scenarios solely in your head. Say them out loud! Actually hearing yourself say your position out loud is much more powerful than listening to it in your head. This will also help spark ideas.
3. Anticipate. Think of the other sides' response to your position and create your counterarguments. Write down bullet points and practice them again and again.

You will *never* regret time spent in the preparation phase.
4. Shadow someone. If possible, shadow someone who is already doing a similar type of negotiation. Don't be shy about asking — they will likely find it flattering. And even if they are bad, at least you learn what *not* to do!

**"LUCK IS WHERE PREPARATION AND OPPORTUNITY MEET."
– LUCIUS ANNAEUS SENECA, PHILOSOPHER.**

One interesting thing I've found about fear is that it pops up in two main situations.

1) I'm doing something new and I'm unsure of myself,

-Or-

2) I'm doing something that *really* means something to me.

If I know what I'm doing and I'm confident in my knowledge, skills, and abilities, there is no fear. I've worked for a company that went through a period of significant growth when it acquired several other companies. Owners and leaders of those companies who were thinking about combining with ours often visited our corporate headquarters for informational meetings. During that time, if someone popped into my office without notice and asked me to address those visitors, I could do so without hesitation.

I could "sell" the Legal Department and the company, field all their questions, and feel 100% confident because I'd done so hundreds of times and I believed in the company. I didn't worry that I'd get stumped. I knew my subject matter, so if I did get a question I couldn't answer, I was always impressed that they asked such a great question! I would tell them that I don't know the answer, but I would get back with them. I never got embarrassed because I was confident I was still the subject matter expert.

If you are a regular at the gym, you don't fear going because you've done it so many times. You've eliminated all fear associated with that action. However, if you are out of shape, haven't been to the gym in years, and are starting an exercise program from scratch, it's natural to have some fear. Fear you'll look silly, fear you won't know what to do, fear of failing.

The next time you recognize that you're fearful of a situation or idea, do a quick body check to notice your physical manifestations. This will help you identify fear quicker when you experience it the next time. You may be able to identify the physical responses before you consciously recognize the emotional reaction to fear. Either way, the most efficient way to combat fear is to notice it, name it, feel it, and most importantly, keep moving!

Imposter Syndrome and Fear

Often the biggest fear associated with learning to negotiate is quite simple: Who am I to "Make the Ask"? People get intimidated that they don't have the education, authority, or insight to ask for new terms in a transaction. These reactions are the symptoms of what's known as the "Imposter Syndrome." The Imposter Syndrome (originally referred to as "Imposter Phenomenon") comes from a 1978 article by Pauline R. Chance and Suzanne A. Imes. It's the idea that many high performers live with a constant fear of being outed as an imposter. A feeling that one day someone will recognize you as a fraud and announce it with a bullhorn.

Naturally, this feeling can generate extreme anxiety and stress. It can steal joy from any situation. While it's influenced by your gender, age, and profession, I have seen this in a variety of people. And it's a common feeling during negotiations, regardless of how people appear from the outside. As a young negotiator, I always had this in the back of my mind. "What if he realizes I don't have 100% of the answers? He'll know I'm faking, and I'll lose face with both him and my client."

It takes practice to overcome this feeling. You have to recognize it when it shows up to the party, give it a nametag, then quietly show it to a chair in the corner. It's here, it isn't leaving, so we need to manage it.

Christy Wright, the successful author, speaker, and podcaster, puts it best when she encourages people to "Do It Scared." I love Christy's invitation to "Do It Scared," because so often we wait to act until we are 100% ready. And are we ever 100% ready in real life? Especially when we are stretching ourselves and growing our skill sets. If you let fear control you, you will not improve. Don't let fear limit your opportunities! "Do it Scared" is an excellent slogan to have visible on your desk. It's a subtle reminder to keep charging forward — regardless of your fear level.

> "I STILL BELIEVE THAT AT ANY TIME, THE NO-TALENT POLICE WILL SHOW UP AND ARREST ME."
> —MIKE MYERS, ACTOR/COMEDIAN.

> "I HAVE WRITTEN ELEVEN BOOKS, BUT EACH TIME I THINK, UH OH, THEY'RE GOING TO FIND OUT NOW. I'VE RUN A GAME ON EVERYBODY, AND THEY'RE GOING TO FIND ME OUT."
> — MAYA ANGELOU, POET/AUTHOR.

Interestingly, there is an opposite to the Imposter Syndrome known as the Dunning-Kruger effect. This is the dangerous combination of a person who has *lower* than average skills and abilities but believes they are doing *amazing* work. The belief in one's superior performance with nothing to back it up. Listen, it's always good to exercise self-awareness. And if everyone in the room is calling you a clown, you should check your shoes! But I imagine this is *not* the case for you. If you thought you rocked at negotiation and had nothing to learn, you are likely not reading this book.

But it is an interesting trait to look for in your counterpart. If you encounter this personality, you will likely have an uphill battle because one of you is grounded in reality, and the other is in fantasyland. My suggestion is threefold: document, document, document. Make sure everything you agree to is in writing so "history" won't be made up later. Send follow-up emails for every conversation and meeting. You will never regret documenting with this type of personality. It's better to over-document than it is to under-document in this situation.

Procrastination

When you are new to negotiation, it can be intimidating. Sometimes it can even seem a bit overwhelming. And what is the best thing you can do when something is uncomfortable, but at the same time important and necessary? Put it off. Ignore it. Procrastinate. It will go away eventually.

Kidding, of course. As you learn these new skills, pay attention to what you are *not* doing. If you know that you need to interact with someone but you keep putting it off, do yourself a favor and pull that Band-Aid® off. Get it done. Jump in. Procrastinating only expends energy on *not* doing something, which is ridiculous and only increases your stress levels. And I should know. While I'm generally a task-driven,

Type-A personality, there are times when I can procrastinate with the best of them. I'm talking Olympic-level, gold medal-quality procrastination.

There are times, I have to admit, when my powers of avoidance are quite impressive. In those moments of weakness, perhaps when I need to have a particularly difficult conversation with a colleague, you'd be surprised how important it becomes for me to clean my office. Like, "Martha Stewart is visiting in four hours for a photo-shoot" kind of clean. Sometimes when there is a call that I need to make that I'm dreading, taking the dogs on a walk is *the* most important thing I need to do at that moment. And thanks to the miracles of modern technology, it's easier than ever to focus your attention on something that doesn't matter. We are a click or two away from being able to avoid a task all day. Netflix, I'm looking at you! You give us five seconds between episodes to determine if we are going to be a productive human or consume a whole days' worth of 90's sitcoms.

Even as a goal-oriented person, you can still fall into this trap. You can make all the checklists and hourly plans for the day, but if you didn't sleep well the night before, if you have a difficult interaction, or if you get stuck on a tough part of a project, it's easy to throw on some headphones and zone out for a little while on whatever internet content you may be drawn to at that moment (news, social media, entertainment). Sometimes a mental break works. But sometimes you lose hours of valuable and productive time on things of little value.

If you get pulled into this pattern, the good news is that there are tools to help keep you on track. There are quite a few programs and apps to "quiet the noise" and help you stay focused by eliminating electronic distractions[1]. The app I currently utilize is called "Freedom." With this app, you can add sites to a banned list during a particular time frame. I chose the sites that I recognized were "black holes of time wasting." I have sessions set up for different times. For example, when I'm writing, I have all "fun" sites blocked from 8:00 a.m. to 5:00 p.m. Facebook, Twitter, embarrassing-to-admit celebrity gossip sites (cough, TMZ, cough again), and all news sites. I also have one session that bans any entertainment streaming sites, Netflix, Hulu, etc. from 11:00 p.m. to 5:00 a.m. so when I wake up in the middle of the night, I'm not tempted to watch shows and get stimulated, thus making it harder to go back to sleep. Instead, I read.

---

[1] As you know, technology seems to change every week. However, there will always be solutions available to stop you from falling down the procrastination rabbit hole. You just need to look for them!

If there is indeed something important going on in the world, the "breaking news" features still arrive on my phone. Or, friends/family will text me when they know I'm out of the loop. If electronic distractions are plaguing you, don't get down on yourself about a lack of self-control. Instead, look for ways to manage and improve the issue. Perhaps you turn off all of your pop-up notifications during times of focus. Because let's be honest, do we really need a pop-up notification that a friend from high school got a new kitten? I'm pretty sure this information will "keep" until you are ready to read it. You can also use auto-replies to let people know you are unavailable. In the auto-reply, you can tell them to call you if they truly need you during a specific time (old school, I know!).

With observation, you'll become quicker to notice any self-sabotaging patterns. With active self-awareness, you'll recognize that whatever you're avoiding is not as bad as what you anticipate. It's better to face it and jump in.

Another tool to overcome procrastination came from an unlikely source — the U.S. Army. The Army's Transportation Corps is responsible for the movement of Army personnel and materiel by truck, rail, air, and sea. While their official motto is the "Spearhead of Logistics," they adopted as their unofficial motto the Albert Einstein quote "Nothing happens until something moves." I laughed when I first read it because it sounds like a big "Yeah, of course!" But the more I thought about it, the more I realized the power behind such a simple statement. If I don't take action and do my part, nothing in my life will get done. And when I'm in a procrastination spiral, that's what I try to remind myself. Just move. Take action. Take a small step. Make it happen.

This is especially helpful when you are avoiding making a phone call. Prepare, write your talking points, and create boomerang responses (we will discuss those later). Then quickly pick up the phone and start dialing. Because it's true. Nothing happens until something moves!

> "THE MOST EFFECTIVE WAY TO DO IT, IS TO DO IT."
> – AMELIA EARHART, PILOT AND MY PERSONAL CHILDHOOD HERO.

The Four Fallacies of Negotiation

When someone tells me why they don't want to negotiate, the reasons generally fall within four categories. All are fallacies and misconceptions.

Understanding these reasons – and why they are wrong – is the first step to overcoming your fear of negotiating.

Fallacy Number 1: "I Don't Have Any Leverage, so I can't ask for anything."

By far the most common fallacy. Leverage is a perceived advantage that one party has over the other. The idea that one side can sway their counterpart because they have some advantageous position. However, thinking that you need "leverage" to negotiate is a self-imposed obstruction.

Would you believe me if I told you there is a tribe of people that have absolutely *no* leverage but get what they want more than not? What would you say if I told you that at one point in your life, you were a member of that tribe?

Children are *masters* of negotiation without leverage!

Children are successful at negotiating deals. Is a child so stifled by fear they won't ask for dessert? Or to stay up late? No way. Kids have no leverage, but they always ask. The fear of hearing "no" is rarely a deterrent to these pint-sized negotiators. They operate with a solid understanding of practical statistics: if they ask enough times, they *will* eventually hear a "yes." Talk about a living example of "Don't Ask, Don't Get."

Real Life Example

When I negotiated contracts for material testing for an engineering firm, we were in a weak negotiating position 80-90% of the time. We could be quickly replaced by a firm providing the same service (although not as well, in my opinion) and the client was typically on a short fuse to get the work done. Being replaceable and having a time crunch certainly doesn't give you much leverage!

Even with those factors, the success rate we had for getting our most important terms was at least 85-90%. How did we have such a high rate of success? Because if you approach someone with a reasonable request and in a pleasant manner, they are more likely to work with you to find a solution. For the remaining 10-15% of projects, we had to make a business decision to take the deal, manage the risk, or walk away from the project entirely.

Another example of leverage-free but successful negotiations involve the "standard of care" provision of a contract. I once worked for a company who valued a specific standard of care because it was defined by their professional liability insurance carrier. Basically, the standard of care says you should be performing the tasks in the same manner your professional peers would be if they were in the same situation. The tricky part is that if you are in a *professional* field (legal, medical, engineering, etc.), you aren't allowed to provide any guarantees or warranties about your services, or you've exceeded your standard of care.

For example, a doctor can't say "I guarantee this prescription will cure you." And if they do, they violated their standard of care and their professional liability insurance would not cover a claim if you said the prescription did not actually cure you.

Consequently, professional service providers cannot have contracts that have any language regarding guarantee and warranties because it would violate their standard of care. This meant that we would have to change "Provider will provide the highest level of service" to "Provider will provide the level of service consistent with the standard of care in the industry." Deleting "highest" inherently looked shady, like we were intentionally going to do a bad job. This was 100% not the case. And I had zero leverage here.

When I requested these changes, I made sure I did so in an uber-professional and pleasant manner. I agreed with their objections and their observations that it looked unscrupulous. I explained in a calm and kind tone that these changes were related to our insurance requirements. And I clarified that if they wanted our services to be covered by insurance, we needed to make these changes. It was actually to their benefit. I also reassured them that if we were manufacturing widgets (instead of providing a professional service), it would be 100% appropriate to demand a guarantee and warranty. After this conversation, it was rare that my counterpart did not make the requested changes.

Fallacy Number 2: "They Won't Negotiate."

If I had a dollar for every time one of my clients told me this, well, I'd be a thousandaire! Unless you have first-hand knowledge from a real *decision maker* that this is true, then you should not assume negotiation is off the table. Remember, "Don't Ask, Don't Get." Until you ask the question, you do *not* know if they will negotiate, so don't fall for this fallacy.

Don't Ask Don't Get Math:

Wanting something + Not Asking = Not getting it 100% of the time.

Thousands of times, I've had a project manager tell me their client will not make changes to their contract. They believe this for one of many reasons:

1. The project manager is afraid that starting a negotiation will blow up the deal or slow it down (or both). So instead of admitting these fears, they present the "no negotiation" excuse.
2. Someone from the client's company doesn't want to work with their Legal Department or decision makers because they are slow or sticklers (or both), so the client's project manager takes the path of least resistance and announces "no changes" even though that decision isn't within their authority.
3. We have tried to negotiate before, and they have made their "no negotiation" position clear.

4. We have verifiable information that they will not negotiate. Perhaps one of our employees used to work there and has first-hand knowledge of their policy. Or it's a regulated industry with no discretion to change contract terms (we will discuss those later).

In business, almost anything is negotiable. You should not accept a "no negotiation" response at face value unless you *truly* know that there is no choice. Are you sure you are interacting with a true decision maker? Is it worth asking again? Remember, "Don't Ask, Don't Get."

Fallacy Number 3: "I Don't Like Conflict."

In my experience, at least 80% of the time people are reasonable, and there isn't real "drama" like what's portrayed in television and movies. To be fair to the entertainment industry, it wouldn't make for a blockbuster if after hearing the "Dun, Dun" introduction to *Law and Order*, they cut to people hammering out the details on the deal they creatively agreed to execute.

There are plenty of books that will describe the formal positions you can take during a negotiation, aggressive/adversarial being one. However, in most cases, people are willing to work with you if you incorporate The Three R's:

1. Ready
2. Relatable
3. Reasonable

We'll go into these in detail later, but don't let a fear of conflict prevent you from asking a question. Instead, I challenge you to reframe this concern. As an alternative to "I don't like conflict," tell yourself "I don't like being taken advantage of," or "I don't want to leave something on the table." This will change both your mindset and your energy.

Amelia Earhart said, "The most difficult thing is the decision to act. The rest is merely tenacity. The fears are paper tigers. You can do anything you decide to do. You can act to change and control your life and the procedure. The process is its own reward."

Preach it, Amelia!

Fallacy Number 4: "It's Rude to Ask, and I Don't Want to Make Someone Mad."

In my experience, if you are pleasant in your "ask" and not a complete jerk, people will not be offended that you asked for changes to their offer. They simply tell you "no." Sometimes they will explain why and sometimes they won't. It turns out that "no" is a complete sentence and doesn't require an explanation.

If you inadvertently offend someone when you ask them to change a term or price, you can explain authentically and politely that you meant no harm. Being honest and polite still gets you a long way — regardless of what the twenty-four-hour news cycle may indicate! We'll discuss areas where you should *not* attempt negotiation in the "Be Ready" section.

Conclusion

- Figuring out your "why" will help motivate you toward successful negotiation. However, sometimes, you still may have strong obstacles blocking your way. I suggest you review your negotiation history to see if you can identify the cause. You may or may not have a root cause, but if you do, often identifying it helps you defeat your personal obstacles.
- We all make excuses, play into fallacies, and let stumbling blocks stand in our way. But if you want to successfully negotiate, you have to try and eliminate your excuses, not give into the fallacies, and knock down your obstacles. Your fear, feelings of imposter

syndrome, and temptation to procrastinate may not go away, but you can fight your way through it by noticing it, naming it, doing it scared, and using technology to help you stay on track.

SECTION II

BE READY

"BY FAILING TO PREPARE, YOU ARE PREPARING FOR FAILURE." – BEN FRANKLIN, FOUNDING FATHER/INVENTOR EXTRAORDINAIRE

"NEVER HALF-ASS TWO THINGS. WHOLE-ASS ONE THING."
— RON SWANSON, PARKS AND RECREATION

Do not underestimate the importance of preparing for a negotiation. When you are well prepared and complete a successful negotiation, you feel like a rock star. Under-preparing and getting run over during a negotiation can make you feel like a rock groupie. One makes you feel great about yourself, your talents, skills, and abilities. One makes you want to take a shower and rethink your life choices.

Preparation sets you up for a successful negotiation. Investing in this step will give you confidence heading into your negotiation and will help you determine what you *are* willing and *not willing to* give up and will keep you on track, ensuring you don't get caught up in emotion. Don't skip this step. Be a rock star.

Areas of Little to No Negotiation

Before you start researching and preparing to negotiate, you need to make sure you can negotiate in *this* situation. You need to make an assessment to see if negotiations are appropriate, welcomed, or allowable. While most situations have some element of negotiation, some situations would be inappropriate to "Make the Ask."

For example, if you received a more-than-fair employment package, I don't advise you "negotiate for negotiation's sake." It is likely that the Human Resources Department has a specific basis for their offer and will know whether it is a generous offer or not. If it's a generous offer, you may be setting a tone of ungratefulness straight out of the gate (especially true if they know your current compensation package, which is likely).

Instead, I suggest accepting the generous package, and after six months to a year, you can consider negotiating additional terms. Then you can point to your "wins" and show how much value you've added in a short amount of time. As a manager, this is much more palatable than if someone tries to nickel and dime you on the offer without a basis to do so.

> **Pro Tip:** I can report with authority that Car Max's "No negotiation" rule is exactly what it says. I tried, so you don't have to!

I also have a strict "don't negotiate with artists" rule. Probably because I have artist-envy, but also because that field is not accustomed to much negotiation for their offerings. So, tread carefully in creative fields. They tend get offended when you request a decrease in pricing. I'm sure it's because they have such a personal connection to their creation. Be aware that you are in a unique area and be sure to weigh your cost versus benefit before negotiating on price.

Same goes with childcare. I'm not sure about you, but I don't want my caregiver to feel that they've been undervalued while they are looking after my child! Plus, it can sometimes be hard to keep your emotions in check when you are addressing the care and wellbeing of your child. Consider this illustration:

From the TV show "*30 Rock*":

> Jack Donaghy: Meanwhile, I just got worked over by my Trinidadian night nurse. I made every mistake you can in a negotiation: I spoke first, I smiled, I negotiated with myself. If I had done that in a mock negotiation in business school, Professor Widmer would have spanked me in front of the whole class - bare bottom!
>
> Liz Lemon: OK, but it's harder with someone like a nanny, right? I mean, there's an emotional component: she takes care of your baby.
>
> Jack Donaghy: Lemon, you just had a structural, analytic insight. Professor Widmer would have given you a "Good Job" spanking!
>
> Liz Lemon: What *is* business school?

I'd much rather make sure someone taking care of someone as important as my son feels they are being rewarded fairly and not "bottom of the barrel." Child care is one area where I want to sure that I've got an "employee" who feels good about their job and how they are treated. Fingers crossed, none of my future sitters are reading this book!

Additionally, industries heavily regulated by federal or state law (utilities, banks, airlines, and hospitals) can be tricky. In these situations, even if your counterpart would like to help you, their hands are probably tied by regulations that require them to treat everyone the same.

However, you can still ask questions to get a better deal.

For example, say you are in a financial crunch and are delinquent on your electric bill. Electric utilities are highly regulated, so many people think that you have no room for negotiation with them and they'll just mechanically shut off your service. But like any transaction, you just need to ask. When you contact the electric company to work something out, ask them about repayment programs over several months or if they have any programs that can assist in repayment of your bill. Many times, utility companies can connect you with a state-established fund to help people in this exact situation.

Regulated industries like banks or utilities often don't have much discretion. Even so, getting them to work with you is all about asking the right questions. Be polite, ask questions, do your research, and you can get help to find the right group, person, or program.

Determining Your What

If you have identified this is an area you can negotiate — and in most situations, you can — you first need to define your "what." What are you negotiating for? What is your ideal end result? What exactly do you need from this interaction to succeed? How are you going to define success for this negotiation?

- Will you be successful if you stick to your pre-established budget?
- Do you need a certain base salary, extra benefits, or more vacation days?
- Do you need key terms for an agreement to meet your company's risk tolerance policies?

Define your goal. Regardless of the "what," it's still a negotiation, and you don't want to even *think* about starting without a clear idea of where you want to end.

Once you know your "what," you need to prioritize all your negotiation wants and needs so you are one hundred percent clear on what you are willing to compromise and what you are not. If you don't know the end game you want in a negotiation, prepare to be embarrassed, or even, witness a complete failure.

Real Life Example:

In my first semester of law school, I moved into a one-bedroom apartment in a great part of town within walking distance of fantastic restaurants, bars, and shopping. I had a great view. The apartment was modern and cool. I didn't have a roommate. It was way better than any cinder-block walled dorm or multi-roommate apartment that I lived in at college. It felt like my first "grown up" apartment. I was beyond excited. Not only was I tackling graduate school, but I was also proving my independence. I imagined myself sitting at my desk, surrounded by thick legal texts, studying 19th century case law, sipping hot tea, and occasionally gazing out one of my windows at my beautiful view. It was fantastic.

Well, that is, until the cockroaches came. And man, did they come in droves!

After a month in my beautiful apartment, a few cockroaches decided that they liked my apartment as much as I did. And they invited their friends. They appeared in the kitchen — even running across clean silverware in the dishwasher. On the floor. In the cabinets. In the bathroom. Everywhere.

I put out some traps, only to realize I was outmanned, outnumbered, and out of my league! I talked to the apartment management and they were, to their credit, very responsive. They treated my apartment several times in one month. Apparently, the cockroaches simply saw my attempts at chemical warfare as a challenge. They rallied, invited even more of their friends, and came back even stronger. When one ran across my toothbrush into the medicine cabinet, it was the last straw. My dream apartment was officially a nightmare.

I stomped downstairs to the rental office (angrily, I might add; we'll talk about managing emotions later). On the way there, I mentally rehearsed my speech. I was confident that I could impress the manager with terms I learned in my first few weeks of law school like "implied warranty of habitability," "constructive eviction," and other marginally-understood legal concepts. (At no point, however, did I contemplate mentioning that I was a law student. And at no point since I've been practicing law have I *ever* uttered the ridiculous phrase "Do you know who I am? I'm a lawyer!" And I never will. And I'd like to suggest, respectfully of course, that anyone who utters that phrase should be exiled from society.) After I rattled off the parade of horrors that was my formerly lovely apartment, my righteous indignation-filled speech was stopped with an apology and one question: "I'm sorry that you've had this experience. What can we do to make it right?"

I didn't know what to say. I was so focused on getting them to *agree* this was unacceptable that I didn't think about what I actually *wanted* from them. They caught me off guard with such a simple question, and I was embarrassed. The ONE question I should have been leading with and using to direct my argument was the one I didn't think about.

After catching my breath and stalling with some rambling nonsense, I finally voiced my "want." I wanted an equivalent, but cockroach-free apartment in the same building at the same price, and I wanted them to help move all my furniture. A pretty reasonable request given the circumstances. They agreed and we all moved forward. My new apartment actually had a better view and was blissfully free from unwanted insect visitors!

It may seem obvious after this section, but always know your "what." Be able to summarize exactly what you want and why. If you can't easily articulate your "what," you may want to rethink if you are asking for the right thing.

Prioritization: Key to Being Ready

You may have determined you have a lot or at least several "whats." Take all of your "what you are going to negotiate for" and prioritize these requests. Here you determine the order of importance for your changes/requests. This is an important step because it will help you determine where you can compromise and where you cannot.

One of the most important things you can do during the preparation phase in order to be "ready" is to prioritize your three types of "haves":

1. Have to Haves
2. Helpful Haves
3. Hopeful Haves

<u>Have to Haves</u>

These are the "asks" you are willing to walk away over. If you don't get these "asks," you have to walk away from the deal. Identifying these before you begin a negotiation is crucial. They will keep you on target and ensure you don't make a "bad deal" by giving up something you needed. Consider these the Nancy Sinatra items: if you don't get these terms, you put on your boots and start walking!

Your "have to haves" should be limited and targeted. For example, if you are buying a new car, your "have to haves" may be the final purchase price. If you have a limited budget, then purchase price is going to be on the top of your priority list. Or, if you are negotiating with a potential new employer, your "have to haves" may be the base salary. If you are buying a house, the amount your bank approved for your mortgage is obviously a hard-stop. This is the stage where you ask yourself, "What do I 'have to have' to make this a successful interaction?"

Make sure you write these down. They are at the top of your list for a reason. There will be plenty of room to compromise and be creative in getting the other two types of asks. If you are really ready to walk out of a negotiation on these core "have to haves," you'll want them limited to the smallest list possible.

Think of the "have to haves" as the best friend you've had since elementary school. A friend who you'd take a bullet for on the battlefield. These are your most important priorities!

Helpful Haves

The next level of changes to prioritize are your "helpful haves." These add a specific value to the terms of your deal. They are less important than your "have to haves," but are still important changes worth requesting. This level is probably the heaviest negotiated. Because this level is adding specific value, you will be more motivated to get creative with this level of changes in order to include them in your final agreement.

If "have to haves" are your best friend, then "helpful haves" are good and solid acquaintances. The friend who you can count on for a regular happy hour or round of golf. Solid people who are good to have around. You don't necessarily call them in an emergency, but they certainly add value to your situation!

Examples of "helpful haves":

1. When negotiating for a house, if there is a specific piece of furniture, garden instrument, patio furniture, etc. that really "fits" the house, go ahead and ask that it be included. Either at the current negotiated price or for a small increase. Be reasonable, but also be bold in these types of asks. These types of asks in a real estate transaction rarely get people too worked up. Typically, they are quick "yes" or "no" responses. However, they would be helpful things to add to your negotiation.

2. In car negotiations, here are a few helpful haves:

    a. Coverage of additional maintenance or a detailing trip after about nine months. I suggest nine months because, in my experience, this is when the "lost fries" start showing up in between the seats!

    b. Adding language to clarify that the number you negotiated is the *total* price. If they try to add silly documentation, advertising, or delivery fees that randomly appear on car invoices, you can remind them of your original deal.

3. With new jobs, it's helpful to ask for some amount of accrued vacation so you don't have to wait months before you can take a day off. Please note, this is harder to negotiate when you are just starting out. It's much easier as an experienced employee because they know you are leaving earned vacation at your last gig.

If you are relocating, you can ask for them to cover your moving expenses, or perhaps relocation assistance for the trailing partner who is making the move with the newly hired employee. This addition will help the trailing partner update their resume, work with a coach, etc. to help ease the professional transition due to the relocation.

Again, this level of "helpful haves" are always adding some benefit to your position and should be easy to defend/explain to the other party. And because you have wiggle room on these positions, you can get creative in how you change them so they're acceptable to both sides.

Hopeful Haves

"Hopeful haves" are the last level of asks in the prioritization of your changes. These are changes that would be icing on the cake. They add some value, but you don't lose any sleep if you give them away.

Examples of "hopeful haves":

1. When negotiating a house, you may ask the sellers to have the home professionally cleaned and the lawn professionally treated before you take possession. These additions would certainly add value, but they are not going to make you leave the deal if you don't get them.
2. In a car negotiation, perhaps you notice they have some cool swag for sale on the dealership floor. A "hopeful have" would be to ask that they include one of those items with the car purchase.

If this group were people, consider them the random coworker who wants to connect on LinkedIn. It doesn't hurt to have them there and they *may* be helpful, but you probably aren't going to miss them either!

So why ask for something that isn't a necessity? Because negotiation is a type of dance. Not a country line dance with prescribed, direct, and specific steps. But rather like a Waltz . . . a give-and-take, one move following after the other person leads. Negotiation requires some give-and-take.

If you only present the "have to haves" you won't be able to give up any items. Therefore, you appear inflexible and difficult since it's *expected* that you will offer up a few of your requested changes as a sacrifice to the negotiation gods. Not doing so makes a perfectly good Waltz turn into an awkward Macarena!

While you are willing to give up several of the "hopeful haves," it's also important that you aren't asking for unimportant or silly changes. Every change you request during a negotiation should have some meaning. You need to be able to defend all changes in a clear and convincing manner. And you can only defend them if you actually understand why you are requesting the change.

When I train employees on effective negotiation tactics, I give them a simple litmus test for checking their understanding of the subject matter. If you can't make an argument in simple language (with *no* legalese!), then you don't know the subject well enough. So go back and strengthen the gap – improve your knowledge. Don't be afraid to ask the dumb questions if you don't know the answer. You need the information, not the optic of appearing smart.

We are all beginners at some point so allow yourself to be a beginner and learn. If not, you risk being exposed as a fraud. And nobody wants to feel like a fraud!

"YOU TRIED YOUR BEST AND YOU FAILED MISERABLY. THE LESSON IS 'NEVER TRY'."

- HOMER SIMPSON, CARTOON DAD AND NUCLEAR SAFETY PROFESSIONAL

(DON'T BE LIKE HOMER!)

Research

Knowing your changes is only half the battle; you need to research and be prepared to negotiate those changes.

Know Thy Subject

It's time to become hyper-familiar with your subject matter. This means doing all your research and homework until you feel confident you know the terms, basis, and specifics of your subject matter.

If you are buying a car, for example, this means knowing what your trade-in is worth and why, and how to explain the basis for your counteroffer. In addition, it's knowing what the new car is actually worth and being able to place a value on any extras they are offering (maintenance packages, extra amenities, etc.). You want to feel so confident in your subject matter that you aren't nervous someone will stump you with a basic question.

Knowing your subject matter and being prepared will increase your confidence going into a negotiation. And when you are confident, the negotiation is less stressful and more successful. When I did contract review fulltime, while some of our contracts were fifty pages long with dozens of sections and a hundred pages of supporting documents, our most common contract was short – only two pages long with twenty-one sections. Having negotiated changes to that document for several years, I knew backwards and forwards what changes I would accept and which ones were deal-breakers.

Consequently, I was never nervous to talk to someone about alterations to our contract. They rarely suggested something I'd never heard before, which made me confident in my ability to interact with my counterpart. In fact, when they *did* present something new, I was excited and impressed! Plus, that allowed me an opportunity to be creative and find a solution, something I always enjoy.

Know Thy Counterpart

Once you have a sound understanding of your subject matter, it's time to perform due diligence on your counterpart. Your counterpart will either be representing their own interests, or those of a company. Consequently, you'll want to get as much information as you can about both.

You can gain knowledge about a company in a variety of ways. Your main goal here is to get a sense of what they are like to work with. What issues do they value? Hot-button items and their past dealings may reveal a pattern toward future dealings.

So, how do you do this? Glad you asked!

Your first stop is to ask around. Utilize your social and business networks to see what information you can gather. Specifically, how have they conducted themselves in previous negotiations? What is their reputation like? Are there specific people you should seek out (and ones to avoid)?

A good second stop is the company website. This is what they *want* the public to believe they are about. Read their mission statement, the "about" section, bios, corporate policies, press releases, etc. You'll want to take this information with a grain of salt since it's tightly controlled and may or may not be representative of the company's true values. But, it is still a valuable starting point. You'll also want to search online for applicable articles that may give you an idea of how the company interacts with people.

Additionally, you'll want to check a company's litigation history. This will help you get a feel if they are litigious by nature. When a company relies on lawyers and the courts to resolve their issues, they are likely going to be difficult to work with — from the initial negotiation until the end of your interaction. If they are quick to take vendors, clients, competitors, employees, etc. to court, this should serve as a warning sign! Which is exactly why you want to know this information up front.

Knowing a company's attitude toward litigation will help you calibrate your approach to the deal. If they are litigious, you will want to make protective contract terms more of a priority. Err on the side of over-documentation in this case. Because if there is a question about the terms of your deal when a problem arises, the contract terms are going to govern your relationship. However, if their litigation history shows they are less likely to use courts to resolve disputes, perhaps harsh contract terms will be less important in your prioritized list. Basically, understanding a company's litigation history helps you determine if you really want to work with them.

To determine a company's litigation history, look at how often they were a plaintiff in a lawsuit. If they are a defendant, someone sued them, which can happen to any company, at almost any time. So instead, you want to see when *they* sued someone, therefore, serving in the plaintiff role. To find this out, you can check several places:

1. A simple Google search using the company name and "lawsuit" and/or "litigation" — Don't overthink it!
2. If you have Lexis or Westlaw access (subscription based online legal research tools), you can search by company name,

again paying attention to when they are a *plaintiff*.
3. If they are a publicly held company, check the Securities and Exchange Commission website at www.sec.gov. It's a good source to find significant lawsuits that the company is engaged with, because they are required to be disclosed in their 10-K Form. It won't list all of the company lawsuits, but it will give you some good insight.
4. Check state court websites, focusing specifically on where the company is located or doing business.
5. Perform a company name search on www.Justia.com.
6. Search government websites such as Federal Trade Commission, Department of Labor, Department of Justice, etc.

If your research does uncover excessive litigation history, then you will want to be cautious. Be sure all agreements with that company are in writing. In a nutshell: document, document, document! You want to be sure you can tangibly prove what you agreed to… and what you did not.

During your due diligence (say that three times fast!), if you have access to Dun & Bradstreet[2], you will want to run a report on the company. This report will give you information about the following:

1. Age of the company and number of employees
2. Ownership structure
3. Risk of bad debt write-off
4. Cash flow risk
5. Payment behavior
6. Bankruptcies
7. Judgments, liens, lawsuits, and Uniform Commercial Code ("UCC") filings
8. Financial overview including balance sheets, profit and loss accounts, etc.
9. Overall business risk (ranked low, low-moderate, moderate, moderate high, and high)

Facebook, Twitter, LinkedIn, Instagram, Glassdoor and other social media sites are also good sources of information to determine the values of the company. Do they volunteer in the community? Are they negative in their postings or positive? Do their comments have an aggressive tone? Have they received recognition for programs/initiatives? Of

---

[2] Dun and Bradstreet is a company that provides commercial information and market data for a variety of businesses.

course, with all social media data, take what you learn with a grain of salt.

It is also worth checking websites similar to Glassdoor.com to read reviews. But don't give them *too* much weight. Anonymity and angry ex-employees tend to inflate the negative comments. Plus, people rarely go to those sites to leave positive comments!

Again, you're trying to establish the tone of the company — what they value and what they don't. This will help prepare you for your negotiation. It will help you predict their responses and help you prepare counterarguments. In the wise words of G.I. Joe "Now you know, and knowing is half the battle."

If you are negotiating a contract with an attorney, it is helpful to determine if you will be negotiating with in-house counsel (an attorney who works solely for a specific company) or outside counsel (an attorney who represents a variety of clients). Typically, the in-house counsel will have a stronger knowledge of the business and will have more authority to make decisions. This will help them be more creative in crafting compromises that meet both sides' needs.

It's helpful to know this information because if you are working with outside counsel and they are being difficult, you can always convey that information back to your contact at the business and have them put pressure on their attorney to "play nice." (This applies to in-house as well, but it's more likely applied to outside counsel.) If the outside counsel is a litigator (which you can determine by researching their biography online), they may approach the negotiation with a more aggressive mindset. Thus, you will want to have a more aggressive strategy ready to go, if necessary.

If you are working with a person who is not associated with a company, you should still do your due diligence. Check social media, Google, ask people in your network and do as much research as you can that will keep you off a stalker watch list. I have a strong "don't be a creeper" rule! The more information you know about your counterpart, the quicker you will relate to them, predict their reactions, and gain information to help you create a solution-based compromise.

If someone in your network knows your counterpart, they can give you extra insight. Having this knowledge enables you to prepare more efficiently. If you know your counterpart has a reputation for being difficult, you can plan to have a more aggressive approach. This is an important step which will help set you up for a successful negotiation.

While preparation is important, you'll want to be sure to not get stuck in this stage. It's tempting to stay in the "preparation" stage too long if you are stalling. Pay attention to see if you are actively gaining helpful information for your position or if you're only collecting random data points. At some point, you need to pull the Band-Aid off and get started!

Identifying Your Company's Values and Culture

You don't just want to know your counterpart's company, you need to understand your own company's values and culture. Sometimes mission statements reflect the values of the company, and sometimes they are nothing more than lip service. If they talk about "respect" but the company leaders are jackasses and they tolerate jackassery, then "respect" is a buzz word the Marketing and Legal Departments agreed would look good in a mission statement.

Unfortunately, we have lots of well-known illustrations of this concept. For example, Enron's mission statement said, "Respect, Integrity,

Communication and Excellence," and its vision and values declared, "We treat others as we would like to be treated ourselves. . . . We do not tolerate abusive or disrespectful treatment. Ruthlessness, callousness and arrogance don't belong here." [3] Yikes. In the case of mission, value, and vision statements, actions speak louder than well-crafted phrases.

To truly understand the values and culture of your company, you'll need to pay attention to their actions. Whom are they hiring, firing, and promoting? What projects are getting funded and what ones are getting tabled? Who is getting stuck in their career path and, more importantly, why? Where does the most attention fall? Are they focused solely on profits? Do they tolerate poor behavior in the workplace if someone is a "producer?" Or do they value a mix of both style and results? Some additional questions to consider:

1. Do they hire the most qualified people or are they hiring their buddies?
2. Whom are they allowing continued employment? Are they tolerating poor behavior because an employee is delivering

---

[3] https://www.fastcompany.com/1836576/4-rules-craft-mission-statement-shapes-corporate-culture

results? This is what Reed Hastings, CEO of Netflix, refers to as "Brilliant Jerks.[4]"
3. Do they have a culture where they expect good behavior regardless of the results you are producing?
4. Do they fire people who are pushing for positive change and growth?
5. Are they allowing people to communicate in negative and harsh tones or is the culture to communicate with a sense of respect?

Considering the answers to these questions will help you identify what your company really wants. For example, if they say "respect" is a core value, but the culture is one that is "results at any costs," then you will want to focus on the tangible results of the negotiation. Hopefully, this isn't the culture you find, but it certainly exists, and it's likely you will find yourself there at least once in your career!

If the opposite is true and the company *does* in fact value respect and ongoing relationships, then you will want to justify your results while acknowledging what you did or didn't do to maintain the relationship with the client, vendor, partner, etc. It's all about being in a position to negotiate in the best interests of the company you represent. And being

---

[4] https://hbr.org/2014/01/how-netflix-reinvented-hr

able to document it and communicate it to your manager accordingly.

Once you identify the key values of your company, you'll want to use those to make sure you are clear on all the major pressure points. A core value for any business has to be the financial health of the company, so you must pay extra attention to sales price and incentives. Understanding your business and how it makes money is key. If your company values honesty and integrity (which I hope they do!), you'll want to make sure you aren't using deception or misdirection to achieve your goals. For the record, this is good advice regardless!

I worked at a company where employees were on construction sites, and they created and maintained a strong safety culture. It was well-engrained, not just empty words. It was embedded into almost everything we did. Starting a meeting meant starting with an applicable safety discussion. Equipment was constantly evaluated to make sure it was the safest version for our employees. Individuals were repeatedly told to stop work in dangerous situations (and were rewarded for doing so). Reporting of "near-misses" was encouraged so everyone could learn from the situation. Pre-task planning became a necessity for all jobs.

While the company once "did whatever it took" to meet the clients' needs, it was able to re-shape the safety culture into one that focused on care and concern for each employee (while still serving clients, of course!). The simple but powerful goal was that each employee needed to make it home safely, every day. Since I knew that safety was a core value for that company, I did two things during my preparation phase:

1. I prioritized the safety "asks" at the top of the requested changes.
2. I didn't make changes to safety terms in our contract, because I knew that they would be non-negotiable.

When you take time to identify core values of the company, they will help keep you on a straight path toward a positive resolution. Core values stay at the top of your priority list. ALWAYS!

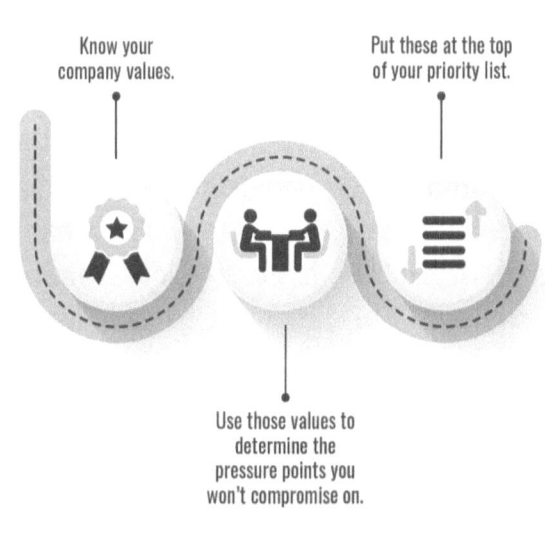

Expecting the Unexpected and Expected!

> "IF YOU KNOW THE ENEMY AND KNOW YOURSELF, YOU NEED NOT FEAR THE RESULT OF A HUNDRED BATTLES."
> – SUN TZU, THE ART OF WAR.

The next stage of the preparation phase involves anticipating the other side's argument and preparing your counterarguments. This is not a step you want to skip. Doing this step can be the difference between looking good or looking like an amateur.

First, put yourself in their shoes. Really slip those suckers on and get a good feel! Think about what their "have to haves" will be. What are *their* most important issues? Is it just price, volume, and making the sale? Do they want to have an ongoing business relationship, or does the transaction deal with a commodity that they can buy anywhere? Attempt to prioritize their position so you can concentrate on the most important issues.

If they are the one making the offer, you already know they've set out their "ask," So instead, after you identify your revisions, you should focus on the counterpoints they will make to your suggested changes. What will their primary objections be and how should you respond?

Also ask what can you offer to make your suggestion more palatable to them?

1. Establishing a potential new client?
2. Completing a sale? Is it time sensitive? If so, you may be able use that to your advantage.

3. Completing the job by a specific deadline? You may be able to use this as leverage. This is not true if the services you provide will *also* be under a tight deadline, so make sure you look at the whole picture.

For example, if a car dealer needs to make their month-end or year-end numbers, one of the best things you can do is start the negotiation close to their due date and walk out when you aren't getting what you want. They are typically quick to call back under these circumstances! However, at the beginning of the month, this move doesn't play as well because they aren't under the pressure of a deadline.

What sort of bridge can you create to connect your position with the position of your counterpart? Can you meet them halfway? When you focus on a creative compromise, both parties will likely walk away with a feeling that they got a good deal — and that's what you want in a majority of situations.

A friend refers to this as the "Pretty Woman" principle. There is a scene in that movie where the main characters are negotiating a "business transaction" in which Richard Gere's character Edward Lewis, a wealthy businessman, negotiated to pay $3,000 for Julia Roberts' character (Vivian, a charming "working girl") to stay with him for the week. This was their exchange:

Vivian: "I would have stayed for two thousand."

Edward Lewis: "I would have paid four."

Both parties felt like they got a good deal. And whenever there is a chance for future interactions, this is important. We will talk about when it's okay to negotiate with a more aggressive tactic later. Spoiler alert: those occasions are rare and, in most businesses, it is almost *always* better to take a cooperative style over a competing style of negotiation.

For those who have not seen the movie "*Pretty Woman,*" IMDB.com summarizes it like this:

"A man in a legal but hurtful business needs an escort for some social events, and hires a beautiful prostitute he meets . . . only to fall in love."

Which sounds inherently better than my summary: "A 1990s movie where a guy hires a hooker who demands safe sex, loves to floss, and cries at the opera. Oh, and they fall in love after he overcame his fear of heights."

But I digress.

You'll want to design your counterarguments so it's easy for the other party to say "yes." This is where using clear communication and being reasonable adds value.

One way to do that is to think about the negotiation from the other person's point-of-view. This lets you stay one or two steps ahead. Plus, it lets you react in a more confident manner, which always projects an air of strength. And sometimes, that's the final element that makes someone compromise a little more or end up giving you what you want.

Real life example:

My son has developed some negotiation skills through his powers of observation (much to my dismay!). His counterarguments at eight rivaled those of some of my colleagues. He knows we have limits on screen time and like any eight-year-old, he constantly wants to push the limits. One day, he was really into a video game and wanted to continue playing. Having lost the "Can I have more time?" argument multiple times in the past, he did what I'm asking you to do:
1. He put himself in my shoes and predicted (rightly so), that I would say "no" to more screen time and would insist that he had to

get outside and enjoy some fresh air.
2. He crafted a counterargument in advance. His suggestion: "If I can have twenty more minutes to finish my game, I'll spend twice as much time outside."

The result? He got to finish the game, and I didn't feel like a terrible parent who is raising a pale, video game-addicted lump who will be living in my basement for the next fifty years. He got what he wanted by thinking about my objection to his request and having a reasonable suggestion to relieve me of my concerns.

Practice

"THE MORE I PRACTICE, THE LUCKIER I GET" - ARNOLD PALMER, PROFESSIONAL GOLFER.

The last step is to practice. I know it's tempting to skip this step, but it is incredibly important if you are new to negotiation. And while it's great to practice arguments in your head, *speaking* your argument will help you improve even more.

That's right, actual speaking. Not Tweeting, Instagraming or Snapchatting or whatever current social media platform is demanding our attention. It's using your mouth to form the arguments. Saying the actual words out loud.

Why is this important? Because when you speak your points, you can often hear the holes in your argument. And sometimes you can immediately hear where you are struggling so that will help you focus on an area for improvement. Also, the more you make the arguments verbally, the more comfortable you will become with them. Even if you are negotiating via email, it's still good to read it aloud to make sure it sounds the way you intend.

It may seem awkward at first, but I suggest you record yourself giving your initial "ask" and your responses to their anticipated pushback. When you play it back, does it sound believable? Reasonable? If not, try a new tactic. Once you become more comfortable with the recording, find a friend and practice on them. It may feel awkward at first, but it will build your confidence and make you feel much more prepared when you are actually negotiating. It is worth the discomfort, I promise!

When I trained new contract review attorneys, I gave them a list of acceptable changes to our standard contract and the reasoning behind each change. I'd have them study them, and then we would sit at a table. I'd then play the "unreasonable/demanding client" and give increasingly nutty requests for changes in rapid-fire succession.

There is no substitute for that type of practical training. I saw those attorneys grow more in those few hours than in multiple days of studying the reasoning behind the changes. You could see them struggle initially and flail for the words or combination of sentences to justify their position. That's when I would double down and press them even further. Once they would become flustered, I would stop the exercise, walk them through the points and counterpoints again, ensure that they understood them, and then started the grilling again!

This exercise wasn't enjoyable for them at first, but each of them said that they were highly prepared for their first negotiation. That tough training experience made the first negotiations seem easy. While the training was tough for them, I knew it was necessary for them to feel secure and confident when they were talking to a customer. I reminded them that it's necessary to "train like you fight." Negotiation is a muscle. The only way to get better is to practice. Dress rehearsals are therefore an important part of getting better!

> "THE FIRST TIME I PRACTICED OUT LOUD IT WAS QUITE A SHOCK. I HAD A GOOD FEEL FOR OUR GENERAL POSITIONS, I'D BEEN TYPING THEM, INCLUDING THEM IN CONTRACTS, THINKING THEM THROUGH, BUT WHEN IT CAME TIME TO SPEAK THEM OUT LOUD I STUMBLED ALL OVER MYSELF. IF IT WEREN'T FOR THE PRACTICE, THAT'S HOW I WOULD HAVE BEEN ON MY FIRST CLIENT CALL."
>
> – PATRICK COURTNEY, ATTORNEY.

Another tool is to prepare "boomerang responses." A boomerang response is a short phrase which tells your counterpart that you hear them, but you are not going to give more information or change your position. These are short phrases you can throw out again and again, hence the name "boomerang response." You may vary the language, but the theme will be the same. They give you a verbal home base to return to if things get heated. Also, they serve as a safe, go-to statement when people are looking for affirmation, and you cannot give it to them.

For example, if you deliver bad news to an employee they may begin to vent about how they disagree or believe it's unfair. Since you obviously don't agree, you can't affirm what they are saying. But you can use the boomerang response "I understand this is upsetting." When you use this several times, they begin to understand they aren't persuading you. You can change the boomerang response and yet keep the general theme with "I know this is difficult to hear." Another boomerang response you may prepare for that situation would be "The important thing is for us to focus on how to move forward."

Conclusion

- The first R is to be Ready. You want to be ready for your negotiation, and that means preparing ahead of time. First, you want to make sure this is an area where you can negotiate. Once you know that, you need to identify what you are negotiating for and what you want the end result to be.
- Then take that list of what you want and prioritize. You will want to ensure your list consists of "have to haves," "helpful haves," and "hopeful haves." While you want to only

negotiate things that matter, it is important to have some wants you are willing to sacrifice.
- Knowing what you want is only half the battle, however. You need to know the terms and specifics of your subject, know your counterpart, and your own company's values and culture. Armed with this knowledge, you can approach your arguments the right way.
- Don't forget there will be counterarguments as well. So plan for those.
- Once you have done all your prep work, you are ready to practice. Practice speaking your arguments and counterarguments out loud, recording yourself if you can.
- While it may seem tedious at first, one bad negotiation where you were underprepared is all you need to make you happy to prepare for your next negotiation!

SECTION III

BE RELATABLE

"I'VE LEARNED THAT PEOPLE WILL FORGET WHAT YOU SAID, PEOPLE WILL FORGET WHAT YOU DID, BUT PEOPLE WILL NEVER FORGET HOW YOU MADE THEM FEEL." -MAYA ANGELOU, POET/AUTHOR

Rapport and Relatability

At this stage, one of your primary goals is to establish rapport. As I've stated, the keys to a good negotiation are The Three R's: being Ready, Relatable, and Reasonable. Developing a good rapport with your counterpart is essential for several reasons. The first and most important reason? People help people they like.

You may consider it unfair, fleeting, and subjective, etc., but it is still true. And if we know it's true, then we can also use it to our advantage. Making yourself more likable to the other party will only help your position. I'm not implying you manipulate the situation so you are trying to trick the other party. I truly believe that establishing a positive rapport, in an *authentic* manner, makes the transaction go smoother.

And while I always look for the best in others, I still need to protect my interests. So if your counterpart is difficult, unreasonable, or challenging, you need to adjust your style. Repeat after me: Do not be a doormat! The goal is to build a rapport by being likable, utilizing a sense of humor, and *authentically* connecting with the other party, whenever possible.

And let's be honest, sometimes, that's just not possible. In those situations, you need to do three things. First, find a way to address the negativity associated with interacting with a challenging individual. Personally, I like to overprepare, visualize positive interactions (discussed in detail later in this section) and also do some breathing exercises prior to working with that person. Second, review your priorities for this to be a successful transaction and stick to them. Fight for your "have to haves." Stay the course and remain as assertive as necessary for you to either a) walk away with what you need, or b) walk away from the deal. Third, keep your perspective. This transaction will end at some point.

I have negotiated with all kinds of difficult people. Rude, unreasonable, unresponsive, mansplainers (men who explain things to women in a condescending manner because they assume they "don't get it"), interrupters, emotional whack-jobs, etc. You name it, I've interacted with them all at some point! And most of the time, I was able to ignore their ridiculous behavior and keep moving forward (after a good venting session to a co-worker to blow off some steam).

Yet, a few times the behavior of my counterpart was so bad that I would recommend a negative consequence because the person was a jerk. Perhaps they were requesting a higher insurance limit, which was in my discretion to grant, but their behavior was *so* objectionable, that the answer was a hard "no." Why? For both a practical and human reason. Practically, this type of aggressive, boorish behavior is indicative of someone who likes to fight and who doesn't have a good filter. If the business relationship goes poorly (on either side), you should anticipate the same type of knee-jerk, hot-headed reaction that they had during the negotiation. They will go from zero to difficult in two seconds. With that type of personality, you need to be extra careful to protect your interests. From a human perspective, because jerks shouldn't win. And while I would maintain my professionalism, still focus on making the deal happen, and would not stoop to their level, I didn't want to give them any "extras" because I didn't like them. It's tough to admit, but this is a natural tendency we all have.

Real life example:

I recently had a plumber examine our kitchen disposal that was working intermittently for a while and finally stopped working altogether. His attitude immediately gave off that "Hey little lady, you don't know what you are doing" vibe. You know the one. The toxic mixture of alpha male and condescension. Knowing that I likely didn't know much about plumbing (100% true, by the way), he spent ten seconds examining the disposal and announced I needed a new one.

"Wait, that can't be right. The house is only three years old, and we haven't been shoving turkey carcasses down there," I responded.

"Well, let me go get a tool and take a closer look." He returned and tinkered with it for less than two minutes. It turned out it was only clogged, and it started right up. We chatted while we waited for the sink to fill so he could flush the pipe. He lightened up and dropped the "big dog" routine a bit.

On the bill he added sixty dollars for a "travel charge" because I was outside of the city limit. Since he didn't mention anything about this on the phone and there was nothing on the website, I pushed back. "We are a mile outside the limit, and you didn't mention this charge before," I argued. He got defensive and started explaining how he had to drive to and from his office and that time was valuable. You know, like I didn't have any idea about how service-based businesses worked! After I gave him my soon-to-be-patented "I'm not buying it" look, he reluctantly offered to remove the charge, which I immediately accepted.

In any other circumstances, if I wanted to use his services again, I might have compromised a bit, perhaps agreeing to pay it next time (first checking with other plumbers to see if it was reasonable) or agreeing to split the charge so that we both got a little of what we wanted. The reality here was that there was no way that I would use his services again. When he arrived, he was patronizing and immediately jumped to the most expensive repair without bothering to examine the problem. The only reason he looked again was because I pushed back. That is not someone I want to employ again. I want to pay people fairly for their work. I want to have long-lasting business relationships with people I trust. This was a good example of someone who didn't even bother being relatable. Instead, he led with condescension. And he ended up not getting what he wanted because he was rude and untrustworthy.

Knowing that people like to help people they like, how are you going to establish a rapport quickly? Luckily, there are several ways to do this and you should try some and see what best fits your personality. Then stick with it. You want to connect with your counterpart as authentically and quickly as possible.

Treat People with Respect and Use Storytelling as a Tool

To relate with others, use stories and treat them with respect. In 2006, my dad bought a 1962 Mack dump truck to use for various activities on his ranch. He's a retired optometrist and businessman and is a "gentleman rancher." I'm not exactly sure where he found this contraption, how much he paid for it, or how it is possibly still running, but my dad loves that dump truck.

If you asked me how to describe it, as they say in the movie Pitch Perfect, it is "Refreshing, yet displeasing to the eyes!" He affectionately named it "Christine" after Stephen King's book. And because the name of his ranch is "Phantom Road," it made perfect sense to have his buddy who did signage paint "Christine of Phantom Road Ranch" on the least rusty part of the door.

Let me repeat, my dad *loves* Christine. He never really needed a dump truck before. But now suddenly, projects were popping up all over town which *required* Christine. He was basically the "Dump Truck King" of his town for the first year he had her.

A few months after Christine joined our family, I found myself at a legal conference in Baltimore, Maryland. While waiting in the hotel's conference area, I started reading signage for other companies that were also having conferences. If you've ever attended a weekday hotel-hosted conference, you know there are certain attendees that seem to appear no matter where you are:

Room 101: An association for something you've never heard of.
Room 205: Some doctors fighting a disease you really don't want.
Room 315: An insurance group complaining about Mother Nature.
Room 407: The national meeting of a company that you've never heard of and can't determine what they do by name alone. Possibly a CIA cover.

As I browsed through the trade show booths in the hallway, I was thrilled to see a Mack Truck display at the check-in area for a trucking conference. I noticed that upon checking in to the Mack event, participants were getting nice sweatshirts and a Mack logo swag bag. And I'll come clean, I secretly *love* bags-o-swag!

As it was close to Father's Day, I started to think how funny it would be to give my dad a Mack sweatshirt that may be worth more than Christine herself. I would be a hero!

When the Mack booth attendants weren't busy, I introduced myself. I explained I was at the legal conference next door (which in retrospect, identifying myself as an attorney may have hurt my position, not helped!). I then explained Christine and how much my dad loved her.

After sharing the story, I cheerfully inquired "Would you happen to have a spare sweatshirt I could give to him —he loves Mack trucks and it would make his day!" The woman who was working the booth did the polite head tilt and responded warmly, "I really shouldn't. But tell your dad we are glad he likes Christine so much!" I responded in the same warm tone, "Absolutely, I'll tell him. And thank you so much for your time. Have a great day!" I then chalked this up to the "win some, lose some" category and patted myself on the back for exercising my "Don't Ask, Don't Get" muscle.

After two days of smiling and nodding at my Mack friend in her booth each time I passed by, she motioned for me to come over. "I'm really not supposed to do this, but we had some leftovers, and I think your dad deserves them, don't you?" I was so excited. "Thank you so much — he will be absolutely thrilled!" And he was. To this day, he proudly wears that sweatshirt while trying to get Christine to start, which is currently running at a 40/60 ratio! The point is this:

1. You must ask for what you want. The worst she could do was say "no" — which she did initially.

2. Be nice to people and treat them with respect, *especially* when you are asking for something! And be courteous when the answer is "no."

3. Never underestimate the power of storytelling. Had I approached her and said "Can I have a sweatshirt?" I'm positive the answer would have been a quick "no" and that would be the end of the story. However, because I took the time to explain the "why" behind my request, it made her want to help me. Again, putting her in a position where she wants to say "yes" instead of "no."

Not Knowing Is a Strength, Not a Weakness

No one enjoys a know-it-all. People relate well with others who admit when they don't know something.

When I'm coaching rookie negotiators, they often get unnerved and unsettled when they don't know the answer. They try to make up an answer on the fly. We've all been there. It's no fun to be outed as not knowing something you think that you should know (remember the Imposter Syndrome discussion?).

But here is the dirty little secret - you can't know everything! And pretending you do will not only lower your likability, it will destroy your credibility as well. Consequently, I have found that if you don't know something, the best thing is to immediately admit it, offer to find out, and close the loop with the information later.

It may seem counterintuitive to some, but acting like you know something when you don't has two potential endings:

1. Your counterpart doesn't know either, and you can fake them out with enough double-talk to where they concede the point and move on. A win for you. Risky, but if it works, still a win.

   -Or-

2. Your counterpart knows the answer. And by trying to double-talk and do anything *but*

admit you don't know the answer, you expose your weakness on that topic. And guess what? Your counterpart will use that against you in some shape or form.

If the topic is inconsequential, they will call you out on not knowing it to undermine your confidence and get the upper hand. If it is important, they will win because you don't know how to defend your position. Either way, this is counterproductive to your bargaining position.

The solution here is to admit when you don't know something, ask for a reasonable amount of time to get clarification, and return with more information. This does two things. First, it eliminates the second scenario. Second, when you admit you don't know something in this context, you appear more confident.

Which person portrays more confidence?

1. Someone who acts "squirrelly" because they can't defend or explain something clearly and, therefore, gets flustered and frustrated. They possibly even become confrontational as they lash out at you because they feel threatened.

    -Or-

2. Someone who owns the fact they aren't sure, admits it, says they will check with others, and get back with you on that issue as soon as possible.

I'd prefer to work with the second person any day. When done authentically and humbly, admitting you don't know something during a negotiation is a strength, not a weakness. So don't be embarrassed to admit what you don't know!

How to Relate in Different Settings

The way you relate to others can change depending on the type of negotiation- if it's by phone, by email, or in-person,

<u>Phone Negotiations</u>

If you are negotiating over the phone, you have a limited window to make a connection and establish your likability. The first step is a simple, yet effective. Smile. Smile when you begin talking with your counterpart. Yes, I'm aware they can't see you smile, but you can hear it on the other end. Pay attention the next time you are on the phone, and I bet you can hear the difference.

To become more relatable, you should consider referencing common connections. You can use social media and your professional network to determine if you have any acquaintances in common. Again, you don't want to turn into a stalker, but if you have a common connection, it can lead to a quick, positive interaction. Be direct, engage in chit-chat, and then get to the point. Phone calls are intrusive so don't go on and on if the person doesn't seem engaged. If they aren't engaging, you are risking not getting a return call later because they will see you as a time vampire.

Pro Tip: Sports can be a great connector and establish a positive rapport. If you are a sports-challenged person like myself, it's helpful to check the sports headlines in the morning, so you are aware of any big games. This is especially true on Mondays. You'll learn enough to get the conversation started. Or at least recognize what they are referencing if they bring it up during your interaction.

And while I am not a sports-oriented person, I have seen this principle in action. In 2015, the Kansas City Royals won the World Series for the first time in thirty years. During the playoffs, Kansas City was electric. Everyone was talking about the Royals. Sporty and non-sporty people alike. It was amazing! So when people would call me to negotiate something and they would open with a version of "How 'bout them Royals?" I immediately had a positive reaction. It inherently made me like them a little bit. And sometimes getting someone to feel like they like you a little bit is enough to sway them toward wanting to help you. They may be more reasonable. And that always works in your favor.

Email Negotiations

If you are limited to negotiating over email, it's a little harder to establish a good rapport. But here are a few tips that will increase your likeability:

1. Using positive, upbeat, and open-ended language. For example, which of these sentences would you react to positively after reading? "You need to make the following changes to the agreement . . . " versus "I'd like to discuss some changes to the agreement . . . "

2. Be succinct. No one likes long emails. No one. If you need to convey a significant amount of information, consider adding an attachment instead of putting all the data into the body of the email. This is especially true when working with executives. They shouldn't have to scroll down more than two–three times

while reading the email on their phone. Otherwise, it may get moved to the back burner. You need to make it easy for them to figure out exactly what you want or need from them. So use headings, bullet formatting and attachments. They will appreciate it (although they will probably never tell you directly!).

3. Pay attention to the formatting of your email. If possible, keep everything you need to communicate in a few paragraphs so it's easy for someone to read when they are reading it on their mobile device. White space is your friend - it makes the email more visually appealing. Bullet points are beneficial.

4. Make your action item clear at the beginning or end (or both) of the email so the other party knows exactly what you are asking of them.

5. Be responsive. There are few things more annoying than someone who doesn't respond to an email promptly. Listen, we are all busy. We all have too much to do and not enough time to do it. But exercising this common courtesy will make you seem likable to the other party.

Of course, there are times that you will not be able to answer their question in detail or engage with them for several days. The key is *to let them know*! A quick email response letting them know you received their email, and you will get back with them on a certain date. Again, this is common courtesy, but it goes a long way in establishing a rapport.

Of course, you need to keep your word and address their email when you said you would. Or if you can't, be sure to communicate that as well. But you can only move that date once. Twice and you look unreliable, like you're stalling, or like you aren't respectful of your counterpart's time. And when you do respond to the email, use an opening such as "Thank you for being patient with my response time." This helps the other party feel more empathic. Everyone appreciates it when someone is self-aware enough to acknowledge a shortcoming.

Pro Tip: When you are working on building rapport and relatability, you need to keep your word. I once worked with a counterpart who was arrogant, rude, and a self-described expert on just about everything, without much to back up that opinion. I immediately didn't like him.

Also, he had a habit of saying he would respond to our requests by a certain date and would miss the deadline. Not just every now and then. Every. Single. Time. When I followed up with him after the missed deadlines, he would offer up an excuse and set another due date where he "Absolutely will get back with you." Which he missed without fail.

The delays didn't hurt my company a bit, but his company lost good business from his delays. It took over a year to get a contract completed which only required insignificant changes. It became a running joke within the company, and his name officially became a verb. If you said "I'm getting Stanned" that meant that someone won't respond and is making false promises. Keep your word. Be responsive. Or you may become a verb. Don't be a Stan!

6. Be professional. Make sure the tone of the email is professional. This includes using appropriate language for your industry. If you aren't sure what the proper tone is for your industry — seek it out. Look for emails that come from the executives and review trade journals. There are style differences between how you communicate in the legal field versus an industrial operation. But if there is a question, err on the side of being

more formal. It's easier to tone down formality than to professionalize something too informal.

7. Get the little things right. Everyone has pet peeves. One of mine is receiving an email that references an attachment, but it isn't included. It drives me bonkers! To reduce the number of times I do this, when I have an attachment, I will not put anything in my subject line until I've added the attachment. So, I've established a failsafe to give me another chance to double check that the attachment *is* attached. It helps to have a checklist (mental or written) to prevent mistakes of this nature. Many email programs use a similar tool when they see the word "attached" and prompt you to double check the attachment is in place.

Also, if you are using an idiom or cultural reference, make sure that you know what it means and how to write it appropriately. My favorite example was when someone wrote: "I don't want to be a dead horse, but . . . " I agree. I don't want you to *be* a dead horse either! But I'm pretty sure he meant he doesn't want to *beat* a dead horse. Getting the little things right helps you establish both creditability and confidence.

In-Person Negotiation

If you have the opportunity to do an in-person negotiation, take it. When you are negotiating in person, you get to consider a variety of elements: mental presence, physical appearance, and nonverbal communications (posture, eye contact, handshakes, tone of voice, etc.) All of these elements help you relate better with your counterpart. Since in-person negotiations involve many elements, I have discussed each one in depth below.

Creating a Mental Presence

The first thing to do before entering into an in-person negotiation is to create a "high vibe." This may sound new-agey and like I'm asking you to wear crystals, sit in a triangle when you negotiate, or practice Reiki. Trust me, I am not. But I do believe that the energy you project when you enter the room (or make a phone call or craft an email) does affect the outcome of the interaction. Consider this example:

Scenario #1: You relocated to a new city, and you are going to a networking event where you won't know anyone. Thinking about walking in the room, you start to feel nauseated. To make it worse, you start running scenarios in your head about how no one will talk to you, how someone may discover you are a fraud, or that you will meet people and they will give you the "You don't belong here," judgmental-look. Your palms are starting to sweat, and your heart rate is increasing.

Looking at the clock in your car, you realize that you've stalled as long as you could and you have to get inside or risk disrupting the presenter. UGH! "I don't want to do this. Well, I already paid, so I have to go inside." As you walk up the steps, you keep hearing "I don't want to do this . . . I don't want to do this" in your self-sabotaging brain. When you get in the room, you are making yourself smaller. Slumping your shoulders, head lowered, and arms crossed. You are not making eye contact with anyone; instead, you have "squirrel eyes," which are darting back-and-forth.

Scenario #2: You head to the same event. On your drive there, you put on some upbeat, happy music and sing along during the commute. When you get in the parking lot, you feel yourself start to get nervous, so you close your eyes and take a few deep breaths. A voice in your head says, "This is going to suck." And you stop that thought and instead think, "I'm happy I have this opportunity to meet new people." You visualize walking into the room with people smiling at you and introducing themselves. Everyone is friendly and welcoming.

You see yourself making connections and feeling comfortable. Taking a few more deep breaths, you head into the venue. While you are walking up the stairs, you intentionally straighten up your posture, move your shoulders back, and lower them down away from your neck. You raise your chin up and enter the room with a smile. You give an authentic smile to everyone you see, and you start making eye contact with those near you.

What kind of presence or "vibe" are you projecting in the first scenario? Confidence, openness, and welcoming? Nope. You are projecting a sense of insecurity, shyness, and distance. How about the second scenario? Similar vibe or the exact opposite? The opposite. You are displaying confidence, warmth, and approachability. If you are an attendee at this event, who would you rather approach for a conversation? Obviously, the person in scenario #2. This is what I'm referring to as "high vibe." It's your physical presence that's conveying a message to others via nonverbal communication about your mental outlook.

People prefer to engage with others who are projecting positive, welcoming energy. High functioning folks are not attracted to negative and wimpy energy. Since your presence is sending a message, you need to be aware of it so you can control it and not vice versa.

So how do you create a high vibe before a negotiation?

<u>Visualization</u>

You can do this in many ways. I prefer to close my eyes and walk through each stage of the negotiation. If I know conflict will occur, I don't try to gloss over it. I'll envision having an intelligent and respectful discussion about the topic and coming to an acceptable resolution. I envision responding confidently and positively, even if there is conflict. I visualize all the way through a complete resolution. Either a handshake, a signed agreement, or turning over the key to a new house or a new car. When you do this and envision each stage, you create an internal calm and strength. A seed of confidence is planted, and it will continue to grow as you cultivate your "high vibe." Listen to music that fires you up. Read quotes that inspire you. Do things that make you feel energized.

Increase your Energy Level

People are drawn to those with higher energy levels. Not "bouncing off the walls" energy, but if you had the choice between interacting with someone who seemed upbeat and energetic or someone depressed or gloomy, whom would you choose? Sometimes, you won't feel very energetic. In those cases, you have two choices. You can try to reschedule your negotiation for a different time and see if you can work around your low energy times. Or you fake high energy. Plain and simple. Alter the things you know make you appear low energy for the course of the negotiation. Listen to music that fires you up. Go for a run or walk. Take a drive and get a coffee. Do anything you know will cause an energy shift.

"DON'T WORRY ABOUT ME. GO AND ENJOY YOURSELF. I'LL JUST STAY HERE AND BE MISERABLE." – EEYORE, WINNIE-THE-POOH, BY A.A. MILNE.

Watch Your Posture

We will discuss nonverbal communication in more detail later, but the next two items that contribute to a "high vibe" happen to both be nonverbals. Your physical presence conveys your mental state and will betray you if you let it. To convey poise, confidence, and an inviting presence, keep your shoulders back and lowered away from your ears, stand up straight, raise your chin, and keep your head back.

The only way to improve your posture while interacting with people is to practice. If you notice that you need some improvement with your physical presence, I suggest the Doorway Drill from *The Art of Charm*:

> "Each time you walk through a doorway make a point to check your body language. Is your head up? Spine straight? Shoulders back? Is there a smile on your face? Are your muscles relaxed (if not, try breathing deep into your belly)? Make the necessary adjustments so you can answer 'yes' to all those questions anytime you walk through a doorway, and you'll have an easy time maintaining confident body language throughout the day."

An applicable and easy drill to help you continually improve your posture.

THE DOORWAY DRILL

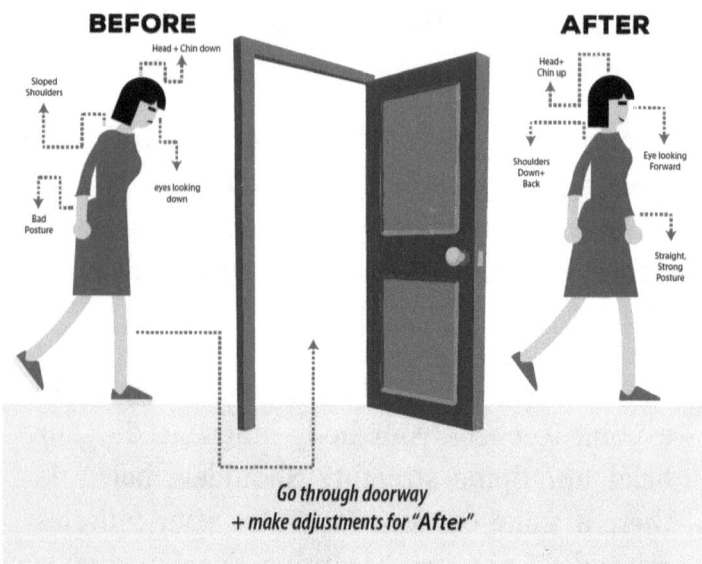

Self-Talk

When the negative thoughts start creeping in — and they likely will — be prepared to repeat a few positive phrases to yourself to stop that line of thought. For example, "Stop it. I'm strong, successful, and unstoppable" or "Nope. I'm happy, healthy, and I'm a great negotiator."

They may sound silly at first, but when you have them available and use them repeatedly, they can help change your mindset to a more positive place.

Boomerangs will also be a helpful tool in managing conflict which we will discuss later.

All of these steps will assist you in getting a "high vibe." But when you are starting out, it may feel awkward to make these changes. This is where you need to have faith, jump in, and embrace the "fake it 'till you feel it" mentality. And that's okay! Everyone has to start somewhere. And knowing these tools are effective will give you the reassurance that you are on the right track. I've done it, and you can do it too.

Physical Appearance

During an in-person negotiation, physical appearance matters. It does. So instead of whining about it, use this knowledge to your advantage.

The first rule about your appearance is to know what is acceptable in your industry. Again, what is appropriate in banking will likely be different in the creative fields or manufacturing companies. If you aren't sure what is applicable in your industry, there are a few ways to figure it out. First, look to see what the senior leaders are wearing. Next, look to those who are getting promoted within your organization. If there is a disparity, err on the side of the conservative dresser. If you still aren't sure, check out industry publications, websites, and industry-specific networking events. Paying attention to your physical appearance isn't about work being a beauty contest, it's about being appropriate for your field and position.

I'm not suggesting you need to mimic those in your industry completely. There is still room for expressing your personality. But if you want to be taken seriously, you need to stay within the general parameters so your appearance doesn't serve as a distraction. The focus needs to be on your negotiation, not your appearance. The theme should be "listen to me" not "look at me."

Real Life Example:

A friend returned to her corporate job after having her second child. She was exhausted and still trying to get used to being a mom of two kids. Consequently, her work life was suffering since it was not her top priority. She was the first to admit that her productivity level was hurting and she wasn't putting in as much effort toward her appearance as she did before she had kids.

After her manager expressed concern that she wasn't "taking her position as seriously as she had once done," my friend knew she had to do something. My friend agreed she wasn't 100% focused on her work at this stage of her life and after this meeting, she knew that she needed to make a change to stay on track.

What she did was so simple and effective, it was brilliant. She created what she referred to as the "Three Prong Approach." First, she invested $1,500 in her professional wardrobe. Shoes, tops, pants, jewelry, etc. all got an overhaul. She planned her outfits each Sunday, taking time to look put together and professional.

Second, she bought three of the most popular management books at the time and stacked them on her desk where her manager could see them. Keep in mind, she didn't read them. She didn't have time! But she wanted the appearance that she was studying the topic since she was in a management position.

Third, she started taking key coworkers out to lunch and asking them about their management styles and soliciting advice for what she could be doing to help in the company. The result? She was promoted within three months. Changing her appearance and approach helped her own attitude, improved her approach at work, and ultimately improved her performance. Once she started looking more professional and taking actions to get more engaged, she started to feel better and her bosses noticed!

Facial Expressions

Facial expressions are a part of your physical appearance. Never underestimate the power of an authentic smile. It can disarm people. It can draw people to you. And it can make someone feel good. Isn't it fun to make someone's day? There is a distinction between "authentic" and "inauthentic" smiles. Most people can tell the difference. But even a strained but well-intentioned effort at a smile can be beneficial because smiles are still welcomed expressions.

Other facial expressions offer insight into your current state of mind. Are you scrunching up your eyebrows, rolling your eyes, tilting your head in a questioning manner? To get and keep a "high vibe," become self-aware of your facial expressions and eliminate those that project negativity.

> ## "WE SHALL NEVER KNOW ALL THE GOOD THAT A SIMPLE SMILE CAN DO." – MOTHER TERESA, NUN, MISSIONARY AND SAINT.

Pro Tip: For a time, I developed a bad habit of crunching my eyebrows together to show dismay, surprise, disbelief, or the "You can't be serious?" reaction. It was to the point that when my husband was delivering bad news, he would sometimes preface it with "I'm going to tell you something that you don't want to hear . . . *please* don't make 'The Face.'" Eventually, because I had to deal with conflict quite often, a crease started developing between my eyes and sticking around even when I wasn't making "The Face." And please keep in mind, I'm usually a smiley, happy person. But years of high-pressure situations, working with lawyers, engineers, and salespeople had started to manifest a presence on my face!

One day, I was in my dermatologist's office, and the assistant asked if I was making a "mean face" often. Yikes. She then mentioned they could take care of it with a little Botox. With an uncharacteristic level of hardly any thought or research, I agreed. A few weeks later, I was putting my son to bed. He was about three and was in the "I'll-do-anything-to-stall-going-to-bed" stage. After countless requests for books, water, snacks, etc., he announced he had to go potty. He was sitting on the toilet, little feet swaying back-and-forth, and I was trying to get him to hurry up and get to bed.

Son: Mommy, are you mad?
Me: I'm starting to get mad, yes.
Son: But you aren't making "The Face"?

While I thought about trying to explain to him the concept of injecting 20 units of botulism into my forehead to erase my work experience, I figured that might not be age-appropriate. Instead, I told him to listen to the tone of my voice and know I was getting annoyed.

And it's worth noting, although the Botox did take away the crease for a time, I found myself compensating with other facial expressions to convey the same "What the heck?" look. So I started getting creases and wrinkles in different locations. Like a game of Whack-a-Mole, I haven't yet found a way not to have my work life show up on my face!

The point? I allowed my facial expressions to feature so prominently in my day-to-day negotiations, it became a permanent feature. So don't follow my lead here!

Nonverbal Communication

If you know what to look for, nonverbal communication can be your best friend.

Real Life Example:

Sometimes asking the question and paying attention to their nonverbals is all you need to do to persuade someone. In January of 2012, I hadn't done anything crazy in a while when I saw an advertisement for a Polar Plunge. If you aren't familiar, this is where otherwise rational people jump in a frozen lake in the dead of winter in the name of charity. In this case, Special Olympics.

Having a good cause and potential for a good story convinced me to try to persuade my co-workers to join the team that we eventually named "Shock and Thaw." My first target was Dave, an easy mark since we both share a crazy sense of adventure. I knew he'd be game and he didn't disappoint. Next, I went to our controller, Doug. Doug is not only the funniest accountant you will ever find (and those are rare!) but also a friend and mentor for over twelve years. We had the following interaction:

Me: With a big smile, I asked: "Doug, do you like children?"

Doug: (looking puzzled) "Yes."

Me: "Then you'd want to help children with special needs, right Doug?"

Doug: (Now sensing I'm going to hit him up for something), "Umm, yeah."

Me: "Then I bet you would love to do a Polar Plunge with me in three weeks, right?"

Doug: "Wait, what?"

Me: "I mean, you said you love kids and want to help those with special needs. So I'm sure you'd be up for the challenge. Think of the children, Doug!"

Doug: After a brief pause, "Sure, I'm in. Actually, I've always thought that would be a fun bucket-list item, but no one ever asked me."

After I had Doug and Dave, I was able to leverage their participation to encourage other colleagues. Keep in mind, both guys were in their late fifties at the time. I approached my friend Vanessa, and said, "Hey, look at what these older guys are willing to do!" Vanessa loves a good competition, so she joined immediately.

Next, I approached our safety manager. I hesitated because I assumed he would serve as the buzz kill since there is a *slight* chance you could have a heart attack due to the temperature shock. But when I listed the participants, discussed the successful history of the event, and convinced him how it would be a fun team-building event while supporting a great cause, he was on board as well. We eventually had a team of twelve strong!

Don't misunderstand - people turned me down. But when I heard them say "no way," I had to do a quick assessment to see how invested they were in their initial response. I was watching their nonverbals as well as listening to their response. If they looked physically uncomfortable and recoiled at hearing the question, it was clear that they were not my target audience. For our IT Manager, Frank, the pure look of horror on his face and high-pitched "Absolutely Not!" was a pretty powerful indicator he was invested in his decision, so I kept walking.

It was even more dramatic when I approached our then CEO. To be fair, he was concerned I would kill a dozen of his employees so I'll cut him some slack. Plus, he did make a generous donation to our team!

But for a few people, their first reaction was a type of eyebrow-scrunching "What?" Since they didn't lead with an outright decline, I kept talking, highlighting the charity; the fact it didn't start until noon; all the cool kids had already agreed to join; and oh, that there would be adult beverages. I'm pretty sure I got a few on that highlight alone, but hey, use all your tools, right? So the take-away here is two-fold:

1. Ask the question.
2. Don't let your fear of rejection get in the way of you doing something great. And watch the nonverbals as part of your process.

Two more things to note about team "Shock and Thaw":

1. In three years, nobody ever died. Thankfully.
2. We raised over $15,000 for Special Olympics in our three-year run. And that my friends, is worth "Making the Ask.'"

When you conduct an in-person negotiation, you want to establish a strong and confident presence. Note: I did not say dominating. Unless you know in advance that your interaction could be adversarial (in which case you would lean toward a more authoritative, assertive presence). You are going for more of a "Don't mess with me because I know what I'm doing" vibe, not "I'm here to kill you and your family" vibe. Big difference between the two.

Think calmly assertive, not aggressive. Establishing an air of confidence through your physical demeanor is a valuable tool because appearing confident in a negotiation strengthens your position and increases your likelihood of success. Therefore, it's important to pay attention to what your nonverbals are conveying.

But when reading the nonverbals of others, please keep in mind that while they can be an excellent way to gain information, they are not foolproof nor absolute. If a person is nervous or intimidated (or both), their nonverbals may project the exact opposite of what they are feeling. But it's important to also consider the context.

I was once hiring a contract review attorney and interviewed someone who had come highly recommended. During her interview, she could barely look me in the eye when I asked her a question. She stared at the ceiling, floor, table, and everywhere else I was not located. Her posture seemed to be making herself smaller as she rounded her shoulders and often crossed her arms or played with her fingers.

While these nonverbals can be associated with a lack of confidence for a job that requires confidence, I thought her physical reaction was probably due to nerves since this was only the second job that she had interviewed for out of law school. I spoke to the friend who referred her for the position, and he said that she was very interested in the position and was in fact a very secure and confident person. She had otherwise great credentials, had great answers to the interview questions, and I trusted my friend's judgment.

I took a chance and hired her, and after a little coaching on this issue, she turned out to be a great long-term employee and highly effective negotiator. Had I only judged her by her nonverbal communications without considering the context, I would have missed a good employee. So again, while reading nonverbals can be helpful, you still need to assess the totality of the situation to get an accurate read on your position.

Pro Tip: Sometimes it's beneficial to call it as you see it. For example, if a person's nonverbals are conveying what you believe is their actual position, you can say "I hear what you are saying, but your tone of voice is suggesting you are feeling the opposite. Is that accurate?" This is a bold move because you are putting them on alert that you are reading their nonverbals, so you are tipping your hand a bit. They will likely readjust to cover up their "tell" but in my experience, unless they are attune to this topic, their body will betray them, and they will fall back into their previous pattern.

Eye Contact

First things first - look your counterpart (and everyone) in the eyes. This seems basic, but you'd be surprised how many people skip this important step. Not only is it common courtesy, but it also projects an air of strength and confidence. Keep in mind there is a difference between maintaining good eye contact and an aggressive or (perhaps worse) a creepy stare. Again, I refer to my "don't be a creeper" rule. If you find your eyeballs are drying out because you are not blinking, there is a good chance you've entered creeper territory.

Good eye contact means you are looking at the person in the eye, blinking, and nodding your head, smiling or giving some other physical clue you are listening or directing your conversation toward them. It's a combination of looking at them directly and also occasionally looking away.

If this is an area you need to improve, take baby steps. First, try to increase your eye contact when you are listening. It tends to be easier to do when you are consuming information rather than communicating information. Active eye contact lets the other person know you are interested in what they are saying, that you are present and engaged.

When someone has what I refer to as "squirrel eyes," eyes that dart around looking at anything but the speaker, they appear disinterested, nervous, and distracted. And that could be the exact opposite of their actual mindset. Looking away and not making eye contact with your counterpart can also convey submissiveness. Don't believe me? Watch dogs. The alpha dog will always hold eye contact, and the submissive, or beta, will hang his head and avert his eyes to the ground. It's quite dramatic. And while we are not canines, it's something you'll want to avoid during a negotiation.

But please keep in mind that some people have conditions which may prevent them from making eye contact including social anxiety, autism, etc. Eye contact, like all nonverbal communications, should serve as a data point to consider and not an absolute rule.

Pro Tip: Pay attention to where your resting gaze goes. It is natural (and expected) to look away periodically when you are listening to someone. But pay attention to where your eyes land. I once interviewed a person whose resting focus happened to be at my chest level. Keep in mind, most women can tell when someone is *looking* there or if they are changing their focus.

This interviewee happened to have this sight line as his default position. But talk about distracting! I found myself trying to move around so I could look him in the eye and started crossing my arms high over my chest. Pay attention to where you gaze is falling when you are not looking at someone in the eye and say it with me loudly "Don't be a creeper!"

Handshakes

Next, a firm handshake. *No dead fish*! There are few things worse than a dead fish (i.e., wimpy, non-gripping) handshakes. I've been told that I look "physically uncomfortable" when I've had to endure a dead fish handshake. Please, for the love of everything holy, do not deliver a dead fish handshake!

Like most things, handshake firmness runs the spectrum. With dead fish on one side, and bone crusher (where it feels like the other party is trying to crush your hand into dust) on the opposite side. You want to be somewhere in the middle of these two extremes, erring on the side of bone crusher if you must.

In general, the pressure should be firm. And a note to my male colleagues, please do not alter your handshake when you shake a female's hand. We can take a firm handshake. We won't crumble or wince in pain. I promise. I would rather suffer through a bone crusher than one second of a dead fish.

Pro Tip: Ask anyone. I am not a hugger. I'm also not an un-emotional cyborg which is what some people think when I say, "I'm not a hugger." In the workplace, I'm a hand-shaker, not a hugger (with rare exceptions). There are just too many ways hugs can be misconstrued or deemed inappropriate. So don't risk it. I've witnessed or experienced the awkward dance of "Do I hug or shake hands?" more than I care to count. It's quite an uncomfortable thing to see! In a negotiation setting, err on the side of a handshake instead of a hug. It's more professional and risk-free. Non-huggers unite!

Physical Presence

You will want to pay attention to your physical presence — the way you are taking up space. This one can be the trickiest of all the nonverbals because if you aren't in control of this one, it will betray you and expose your true feelings without your consent. This is also one area that if you are intentional, you can absolutely "fake it till you feel it." There have been studies that show when you act confident; your confidence actually does increase. Turns out "grin and bear it" was good advice after all.

Remember what it looked like to have confidence? Shoulders back, head up, chin parallel to the ground and a smile. If you don't feel confident, just adjust your body posture to "fake it till you feel it."

But be aware, the pendulum can swing in the wrong direction on this one too. Enter: Manspreading. Manspreading is when a person takes up more space than what is appropriate, typically with wide-open legs and elbows/arms to match. And while it traditionally focuses on men, I've seen women doing it as well — mainly with conference room tables. They spread their papers, materials, and bags in a larger than appropriate manner. Manspreaders are easy to spot, and personally, I think it projects insecurity. To me, it looks like they are trying too hard to appear alpha-like. It reminds of Margret Thatcher's quote: "Being powerful is like being a lady. If you have to tell people you are, you aren't."

I usually recognize a manspreader as a data point and keep moving. Although sometimes, *sometimes*, I will mimic the behavior slightly to convey more confidence in the negotiation status. I will spread my papers out wider than usual on a conference room table and sit back in my chair with my shoulders back and arms on the chair or open on the conference table. Again, keeping a significant presence can convey a sense of comfort and confidence that can contribute to the tone of the negotiation. But be careful to not overdo it.

The next time you are in a meeting, having a difficult conversation or talking to a coworker, pay attention to your body language. Are you making yourself small and shrinking away from the person or are you comfortable, with a positive, confident physical presence? Height can play a role here as well.

I'm 5'10" without heels. So when I'm wearing heels, I'm over six feet. I've realized that I have subconsciously (now intentionally) used my height differently with certain people. I once worked with an executive who was great at his job, funny, kind, and an all-around great leader. He also happened to be approximately 5' 6" tall. When we were standing in a conversation, in an effort to make him comfortable, I stood back and changed my posture to lean back a bit so I was lower. Thus, making me closer to his size and not looking down on him.

In contrast, I also had a co-worker who was approximately 5'7" and was what I could only describe as a weasel. I believe the weasels from "Who Framed Roger Rabbit?" were inspired by this guy. Always looking for an angle and manipulative, he used the "fake charm" routine with female coworkers. He was only nice to you when he needed something and was quick to throw you under the bus at any opportunity. Sounds like a gem, right?

I realized after several unpleasant interactions with Mr. Weasel that I moved closer to him and looked down on him when I was making my point. It's as if my body language was saying "Hey, I'm not taking s*$# from you" versus my reaction with the executive "I want to make you more comfortable."

And while height can be a tool, I don't want my vertically challenged friends to worry. I've met plenty of short people who command a room with their physical presence. My grandmother was one. At 5'2", she wasn't looking down on many people.

But her spirit, smile, vocabulary, radiance of kindness, and perfect posture made her stand out in any room. And for the record, Madeline Albright is 4'10," and she did fine negotiating with world leaders. And guys, Napoleon was 5'2". Height is a tool you can use if it's an option, but if it isn't, it's not a deterrent if you don't allow it to be.

Silence and a Smile

One of the most effective tools during a negotiation is a combination of two undervalued reactions. Silence and a smile. The use of silence is an incredible tool. And one my fellow extroverts would be wise to practice more. It's like a muscle - you need to be aware of it and flex it so when you use it, it works for you. It's my experience that when used correctly, silence is effective at getting your counterpart to unconsciously start or keep talking, both of which are to your advantage.

People don't like long periods of silence. When they feel the silence is going too long; they will start to fill it. And most of the time, they will fill silence with additional information or details regarding their positions. So, when used strategically, you can use silence to gather more information.

When you couple silence with an authentic smile, people are even more likely to continue talking because they sometimes interpret your smile as encouragement or agreement (which may or may not be true). Also, it's common for people to start filling the silence with their own insecurities during a period of silence because they are uncomfortable.

Don't believe me? Try it the next time you are having a discussion with your partner or spouse. I can almost guarantee that they will continue talking and likely will disclose more than they intended when you pair silence with a smile. But I would be remiss if I didn't again engage the "don't be a creeper" rule here. You don't want to stare someone down like a sociopath while completely going mute. But choosing to be tactically silent while maintaining a positive, or neutral, facial expression can assist you in getting more information from you counterpart.

"SILENCE IS ONE OF THE HARDEST ARGUMENTS TO REFUTE." - JOSH BILLINGS, WRITER/HUMORIST.

Learn Your Body Language

It helps to know, understand, and control your body language. One tip is to set a timer that will go off at various points in the day. When it rings, stop to evaluate your mental state and physical presence. Over time, you'll start to become more aware of how your thoughts are influencing your body language. Awareness will bring the ability to manage your body language better. For example, if your timer goes off and you check in while you are relaxed, notice how you are sitting. You may be sitting farther back from the table, your shoulders may be lower, and your facial muscles may be more relaxed. Those are all things you can consciously do to influence your mental state when needed. Sitting further back from the table and intentionally relaxing your shoulders may help you feel more relaxed mentally.

On the flip side, if your timer goes off and you are stressed or upset, you may notice your shoulders are higher and tight, your hands are clenched, and you are clenching your jaw, etc. This is also helpful to know because when you feel these reactions manifest during your negotiation, you can catch them and reverse your response so you can either manage your mental state or not give away your true feelings (if that's your goal).

Another resource is Amy Cuddy's TED Talk titled "Your Body Language Shapes Who You Are." Ms. Cuddy is a social psychologist and associate professor at Harvard Business School. She explains how holding a big, powerful pose for two minutes can make you feel more powerful. In her study, the participants who engaged in "high-power" poses for two minutes had increased testosterone levels, lower cortisol levels (a stress hormone), and had a higher risk tolerance than before the pose.

She summarizes it with this quote, "Our bodies change our minds and our minds change our behavior and our behavior changes our outcomes." Since you will be more successful during negotiation if you feel confident and powerful, perhaps standing like Wonder Woman or Superman in the bathroom before you head to the conference room should be part of your preparation checklist!

Conclusion

- Your primary goal in being relatable is to build rapport, or in other words make yourself more likable. However, this doesn't mean you let others walk all over you. You may need to adjust your approach if you are dealing with someone who acts unreasonable. But for the

most part, you want to remain likable and relatable.
- There are many ways to do this and it often depends on the type of negotiation — whether it is via phone, email, or in person. Regardless of the type of setting, using stories, respecting the other person, and admitting when you don't know something go a long way in building rapport.
- When negotiating over the phone, try to connect with the other person and remember to smile (even though they can't see it, they can sense it). For email negotiations, you want to ensure you use upbeat, concise language and respond quickly. When you can, you want to negotiate in person. In-person negotiations do require the most work in terms of building rapport, but they are the most advantageous.
- To prepare mentally, visualize, increase your energy, watch your posture, and establish some positive self-talk. And be mindful of your physical presence and nonverbal communication. Watch your facial expressions, your level of eye contact, how you take up physical space, and your body language. Ensure that these aspects of your physical

presence and nonverbal communication match your message.
- And as you negotiate, don't forget to utilize silence and smile – it's a great secret weapon.

SECTION IV

BE REASONABLE

Being a reasonable person should be everyone's goal in life! In negotiations, being reasonable (or at least appearing reasonable) is possible even when you are focused on achieving your goals. Appearing reasonable puts people at ease, and, therefore, they will be more likely to help.

So how do you present yourself as reasonable during a negotiation?

Have Reasons to Back Up Your Requests

Don't ask for anything you can't justify. Every single thing you request needs to have a reason. The reason may not be important, but it still needs to exist. Never ask for something you can't justify. Even with your "hopeful haves" we discussed earlier.

To do this, you need to know what you are asking for and why you are asking for it -backwards and forwards.

It doesn't matter how well you relate to the person, how great your stories are, or how charming you may be if your requests are unreasonable and unsupported.

Managing Emotions

Blowing up and getting visibly angry at someone is never reasonable. But there is no getting around the fact that negotiation can often stir up a combination of emotions. Those include, but are not limited to:

Excitement
Boredom
Confidence
Uncertainty
Frustration
Satisfaction
Elation
Disappointment
Enjoyment
Vulnerability

And these are only a few to start. However, it's essential to keep your emotions in check during all stages of negotiation. Why? Because losing your cool is counter-productive most of the time. If you lose your mind and go "howler-monkey crazy" on someone during a negotiation, your counterpart will assume one of the following:

1. You may or may not be off your medication.
2. You don't know what you are doing.
3. You are too volatile to complete the negotiation.
4. You are too high maintenance and not worth the hassle. This may be a trigger for them to ask to work with someone else in your company (if you are lucky). Worst case, they think that you represent the way your entire company will act, so they shut down the negotiation and walk away.

So, does that mean you should always remain completely monotone and neutral in your word choice, tone, volume, and gestures? Absolutely not. And going to that extreme may also make you look like a crazy person. You want to vary all these things to a degree, depending on the status of your negotiation. Be human. However, if you choose to show real emotion, whether it is frustration, anger, passion, etc., you want to make sure you are doing it intentionally and not reactively. You want to know you are intentionally using your emotions rather than being surprised you had an emotional outburst. Big difference!

Not only do you want to remain in control of your emotions at all times, but often, remaining cool in an intense situation can be quite the advantage.

I have a special affinity for Volvos, we've owned two, but we recently moved to an area without a Volvo dealership. So, every time I needed specialized service on the Volvo, I had to drive four hours to the dealership. No big deal, because I would always time the trip for when I was visiting friends or going to events.

One time, I went back for an event and dropped my car off for service and a few repairs, which allowed the dealership four days to get everything done. One item to fix was a faulty rear headrest that was stuck at a 90-degree angle. Plenty of time to fix that and do an oil change and rotate tires, right?

I let the service department know that I was from out of state and I was leaving on Saturday. I called ahead on Friday, but I kept getting voicemail and they didn't return my calls. Same thing on Saturday morning. Finally, I had a friend drop me off at the dealership on Saturday morning. When I went to the service desk, the employee said "Oh sorry, we just got it up on the rack, and we just realized that we aren't going to be able to get the service or the repair done today." *What the what?* Four days and they hadn't touched it.

Apparently, even the Botox couldn't cover up the look of horror on my face because he immediately started apologizing and hanging his head while saying they were short-staffed and they've been running behind for weeks. I was mad, but this gentleman was doing his best and knew that he had failed. There was no point in throwing a fit, which rarely improves the situation and simply isn't my style, but I told him how disappointing and inconvenient this was. I told him how I understand being short-staffed and the challenges that can bring, but they should have at least let me know the status.

He agreed and was apologetic. I let him know I had to head home so they brought the car around and I left. But a funny thing happened as I rounded the block. I looked in the rearview mirror and saw that stupid headrest stuck at 90 degrees, and I got mad! I started thinking how it would be six weeks before I could get back and that meant every time I dropped my kiddo off at school, he had to duck under the headrest from the other side of the car because he couldn't sit in his usual seat. As my blood pressure began to creep up, one word came to the front of my mind - No. No, I'm *not* going to accept this and head home. I'm not accepting this as the final result.

I circled the block and pulled back into the dealership. I took a few deep breaths and mentally outlined a few talking points and then headed to the showroom floor. I calmly asked to speak to the manager and made sure I did so with a smile. When he came out, I explained the situation in a calm, collected demeanor. When he heard the details, his response was "Wow, that's terrible. I bet you're really mad!" This made me laugh, and I responded "Well, I'm trying not to be! Listen, I work with customers as well, and if they had a terrible experience, I would want to know as a manager because I can't fix what I don't know. Your service guy was polite, but the situation seems to be out of his hands if it's due to staffing. I'm here to give you the opportunity to make this right."

He visibly seemed relieved to see that I was not yelling at him in the middle of the dealership. He responded, "I'm going to make this right. Let's get you a free courtesy car to drive home and use until we fix your car. So you don't have to drive all the way back to pick up your car after we fix it, we'll have one of our employees drive your car to your house, then he can take our courtesy car back. That will save you the four-hour trip here and back. Does that sound good?" Umm, yeah, sounds great! Within fifteen minutes, I was headed home in my courtesy car, and two days later, they brought my car to my house.

This was a successful negotiation for two reasons. One, when I started to get angry, I realized I felt I had been wronged and didn't like it. As a result, I needed to process that emotion before I could negotiate and lay out my issue in a clear, calm, but compelling way. Second, because I controlled my emotions and didn't approach the manager like a howler-monkey, he was appreciative and, therefore, willing to find a solution to the problem. If I had been emotional and angry, he probably would have gone on the defensive. Instead, offering him the "opportunity to make it right" gave him the ability to save face after a clear fumble and solve the problem.

As I mentioned, I don't want you to be an emotionless robot. Be aware of your emotions, control and harness them, and use them <u>intentionally</u> instead of with a reaction to an unpleasant stimulus. Being both passionate and persuasive are not mutually exclusive!

Of course, being too attached to your desired outcome can also cloud your judgment in a negotiation. One of my favorite illustrations of this point is the story of our Golden Retriever, Gunner.

We once had a fantastic dog, Trooper. He was rescue mutt. Well, technically he was a Golden, Chow, Dalmatian, Boston Terrier, Pomeranian mix - we DNA tested him. We enjoyed almost thirteen years with Trooper before he suddenly passed away from a medical condition. We were all heartbroken. Our other dog, Scout, missed his buddy and was as depressed as the rest of the family.

After a few months of grieving, my son's teacher mentioned that she had visited an amazing litter of Golden Retriever puppies and we should take a look. She told me that because the puppies were getting older, the seller was discounting his price from $1,200 to $400. The seller was a charming and slightly eccentric retired teacher who had bred Goldens for thirty years. Before our visit, I tucked $400 into my purse "just in case" we happened to find one we liked.

When we arrived, we were the center of a "puppy tornado" with three adorable puppies jumping, licking, and loving on us. One pup clearly stood out. It's true that you don't pick dogs, but dogs pick you! While we were playing with them, the breeder was telling us how it's hard to live on a fixed income, how he loves breeding dogs to make families like ours happy. My husband then asked him how much they were. "$450" he replied. *What now?*

I knew he told my son's teacher $400. But I was emotionally tied to leaving with that puppy. As a long-term, experienced negotiator, you can predict my immediate response to get the price at or below $400, right? Well, you're wrong. I caved. Immediately. I asked my husband, "Ummm, honey, do you have fifty dollars?" No hesitation or counter offer. There was no way I was walking away from that puppy. And I wasn't going to try to haggle over fifty bucks with a retired teacher who was just complaining about his finances (even if he was using that to gain sympathy for the deal. He could have been a master negotiator!). We were getting a good deal anyways ($450 compared to $1,200), I was too emotionally engaged, and frankly I wouldn't have felt good about "winning" by knocking the price down more.

My point is this — if you can't keep your emotions in check, you won't be able to make a compelling negotiation, you won't be able to stick to your "have to have's," so you should find someone to negotiate on your behalf. Perhaps that negotiation should have been one that my husband should have handled (although he generally prefers me to negotiate deals because I love it!). But when it comes to puppies, perhaps negotiating from the heart is okay.

Volume, Tone of Voice, and $%*'ing (Cursing)

Keeping a reasonable volume and tone of voice is important. Sometimes the tone and volume of your voice are all you need to convey a message. By nature, I am not a person who yells. I don't like loud noises, and I hate being around people who yell to be heard. It reminds me of the Henry Rollins quote: "You can't get your head around something if you're yelling."

However, there have been times during a negotiation when I feel a person is not listening. They are either continually interrupting or are speaking to hear themselves speak, and they are not hearing what I'm saying. That's when I change my tone and volume of my voice. I still don't yell, but I will raise the volume of my speech and lower my tone of voice to convey authority. I drop my tone because I find that a high-pitched, raised voice sounds hyper-emotional and unsteady.

The opposite can also be true — when emotions are running high, you can speak quieter to force the person to listen. I'm not talking about faking a whisper so they have to lean in to hear you. I just mean don't engage in the battle of raised voices and instead, lower your voice a little. Changing the volume can be helpful as it serves to disrupt the path of escalation.

Both solutions have merit, and you may find yourself trying both, testing to see what works best with both your counterpart's and your personality. You can only do this when you've established yourself as an even keeled and reasonable person. If you lead with "howler-monkey" volume and tone, you are immediately putting your counterpart on the defensive and their guard goes up. That is setting a negative tone, and that rarely is beneficial in the long run!

Cursing is another tricky topic. You probably assume I will say not to curse under any circumstances. And in general, you should listen to your mother's advice and not use bad words. However, there are times where intentional cursing can be advantageous. I'm not talking foul-mouthed, make-a-sailor-blush type of cursing. Instead, a well-placed, first-tier curse word can serve as a clue to your counterpart that you are serious or getting frustrated (if that is what you determined you want to convey) or it serves as a verbal disrupter.

One of my favorite examples of this is Tony Robbins. Yes, the self-help giant, author, entrepreneur, and speaker with the huge smile is a great curser. In the documentary *"Tony Robbins: I am Not Your Guru,"* it is shocking to hear him frequently drop F-bombs in his speech to a packed hotel ballroom audience. His says that his intentional use of provocative language jolts participants out of their status-quo and gets them to a more authentic place.

Assuming that you are not a multi-millionaire like Tony Robbins who can set some of his own rules, cursing can still be a strategic tool, but one that should be wielded carefully. If you swear too early or too often, you risk being seen as crass and unprofessional. However, there is a sweet spot where you've already established yourself as professional and trustworthy, but you need to "shake things up" a bit to get some attention.

When I teach classes on topics such as contract law or employment law (what some consider boring, but I think are fascinating!), sometimes I get animated and excited and will intentionally say something like, "If you want to avoid a shitstorm, be sure you do XYZ." I can watch as people have a physical reaction to such an atypical word choice - and most of the time it is one of surprise, not of horror.

However, I only do this among groups whom I know, or they know me. That way, the baseline of professionalism and trust has already been established. In that environment, it's more of a funny "Whoa, I was not expecting that!" versus a "How dare she?" reaction while clutching their pearls and looking for the nearest fainting couch.

And keep in mind, if you utilize a well-placed curse word, make sure it is very rare. Continuous cursing may make you look too emotional or uneducated since it is viewed as "lazy language." And consider your geographic environment — some areas of the country are more accepting of curse words than others.

Again, I'm not advocating you freely and frequently curse. Quite the opposite. However, it can be a helpful tool when used correctly. And of course, you'll want to know your audience. Did I curse when I was negotiating contracts with churches? Hell no (see what I did there!). But if I had an ongoing negotiation with someone where we had built a solid rapport and I needed to shake things up to get additional attention, perhaps a swear word would be in order. But again, know your audience. And remember that this can be risky, so be sure that the benefit outweighs the risk.

Also, I have two rules related to cursing that I never break. First, never resort to name calling. On any side. Don't call your counterpart a name and don't call any of your teammates' names. Doing so is unprofessional and downright juvenile. You lose any credibility you were able to establish. Immediately.

Second, never put a swear word in writing. For whatever reason, a curse word seems crasser and more objectionable when in writing. But mainly, don't put it in writing because it's something that you don't want to see later if the deal goes poorly. Emails and memos are where you want to use the CEO test. If your CEO had to read your email in front of the entire company, would you be okay with the contents? If the answer is "Oh, F&^% no," then you should re-draft the email. And this time, leave out the swear words.

Don't Negotiate Against Yourself

Part of being reasonable is being reasonable with yourself. At first glance, this subtitle seems like it should be filed in the "Yeah, no duh" file. But, you'd be surprised how many times you will be asked to do precisely this — negotiate against yourself. Remember back to the rules of construction of a contract?

RULES OF CONTRACT CONSTRUCTION

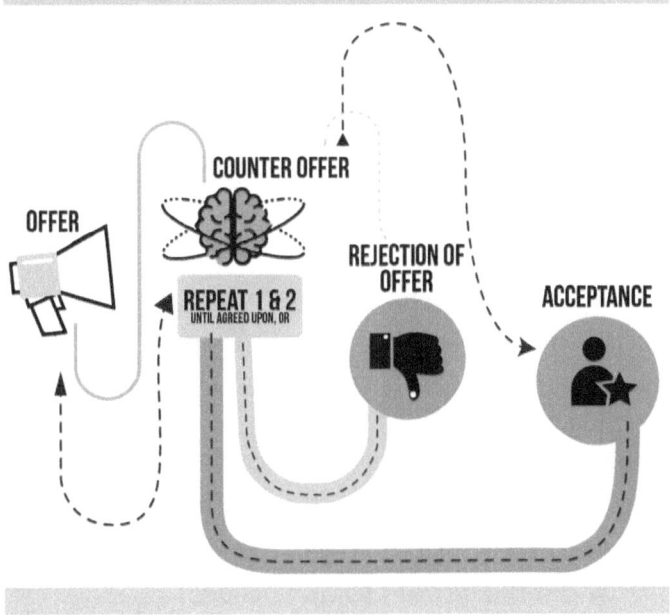

Here are a few examples of basic contract construction:

Example 1:

Offer: I'll buy your car for $5,000.
Counteroffer (none): Sure. Sounds fair.

That was an acceptance of the offer, so a verbal contract was formed immediately.

Example two.

Offer: I'll buy your car for $5,000.
Counteroffer: I'll take $5,500.

That counteroffer rejected the first offer. If the seller said, "sure," a contract was formed. If he said "no," there is no deal.

If you make an offer/counteroffer, *do not* make another offer/counteroffer until the other party makes one first. Here are real life two examples.

I was recently working with a car salesman, TJ, to purchase a new car. I wasn't in a hurry and I knew I had an advantage since it was the end of the month, so he would likely want to make a deal.

I visited the dealership one afternoon, and after a test drive, I let him know that I'd think about it. I told him that I assumed there was some wiggle room on the sticker price since dealerships use sticker prices as a general starting point. He admitted that the sticker price wasn't the official "offer," so I told him to send me his actual asking price. While I didn't counter with a specific price, asking him to send me his actual asking price (instead of the sticker price) was technically a counteroffer to the originally-listed price.

The next day, I started getting text messages from TJ. TJ's emojis are all accurately portrayed.

> TJ: "Really would love to make you a great deal on that car. Let me know what you are thinking."
>
> Me: "Go ahead and send me your actual asking price and I'll consider it."
>
> TJ: "Well, where do you need to be? :) I'll see if I can get my manager to go there. :)"
>
> Me: I'm not negotiating against myself, silly! Just let me know your offer since we agreed it wasn't the sticker price.
>
> TJ: I know. :) That's what I was asking you to do. :) Most of the time, I can do best if I have an offer to take my manager. :) If I know what you're willing to offer, I'll call him and see if I can get him to take it. :)
>
>> Comment: I appreciate him agreeing that he wanted me to negotiate against myself here. It validated my point. Yet, I also appreciate the fact that he gave a reason for why he was asking for a specific dollar amount, and that reason was logical.

This is where I relied on silence as a strategic tool. I didn't respond to his last text. To be fair, I had told him I would be in meetings, so he knew I would be unavailable for long stretches of time. The texts started up again, a day later at 1:00 p.m. on Wednesday:

TJ: What if I can do $2,000 off if we can close the deal today? :).

> Comment - The silent treatment saved me $2,000. If I could make $2,000 for shutting my mouth for one day, I'd be quiet more often!

Me: Unfortunately, I don't have enough time to do additional research to determine if that's a good deal. But thanks for offering.

TJ: No problem. Here is the NADA (National Automobile Dealers Association) printout to help with research :).

> Comment: TJ did two great things here: 1. He didn't accept the first "no." 2. He acknowledged the problem I had regarding research and attempted to eliminate it as an issue by providing additional research. Kudos to TJ here!

I waited a few more days and then got the following message from TJ on July 3rd:

TJ: Hey Lynn, I'm open today if you'd like to come check out this nice car some more :) I will be closed tomorrow though. :).

Me: If you could do $xx, xxx total, I can head your way in thirty minutes. Otherwise, I think we are too far apart, and I'll need to pass.

TJ: Lynn, I would so much love to have your business! I asked the owner, and I can do $x, xxx OFF the NADA Value of the car. What do you say? Want a new car to celebrate Independence Day??? :)

> Comment: He gets points for his sense of humor and comedic timing for connecting a new car purchase with celebrating Independence Day. And, for the heartfelt "I want to do business together" sentiment.

Me: I'd love to, but I'm 100% set on $xx, xxx. But thanks for checking and have a great 4th!

TJ: Maybe we'll get one in with more miles I can call you on. :) What colors would you consider? And Happy 4th!!!

We continued to text about other options, and ultimately, I found a better fit at a different dealership and let him know I was no longer in the market. However, I use this as an illustration of several points:

1. This was a civilized negotiation and at no point was there any confrontation.

2. I made the "ask" in the form of a counteroffer and would not negotiate against myself. If I didn't ask him to give me his best price (after he acknowledged there was wiggle room), I could have either rejected his offer and left, or accepted their offer and overpaid for the car.

   Also, note that I know asking them to give me a better price without first giving them a dollar amount as a counteroffer may be interpreted as me asking them to bid against himself. But since he confirmed there was in fact room for improvement in the price, I felt it was appropriate for them to tell me what that looked like before I make a specific dollar counteroffer. And, while my advice is to not negotiate against yourself, if you can get others to do it, that's a win for you!

3. TJ did a great job not accepting the first "no" I threw his way.

4. He also added value by seeking to eliminate the issue I said was holding me back — lack of research. This problem-solving tactic was helpful. He was putting me in a position to say "yes."

5. My delayed response to his text resulted in a $2,000 savings. Nothing but silence prompted that change.

6. His persistence revived the negotiation. Had he not reconnected and checked in on the 3rd of July, I wouldn't have contacted him again.

7. I appreciated his willingness to help and positive attitude.

8. Although it appeared unsuccessful because he didn't make the sale, I would l00% return to him when we are in the market again. He built a relationship that may benefit us both in the future.

Another "don't negotiate against yourself" scenario involves the negotiation of a salary. I had made an offer to a potential employee, which was fair, matched his experience, and was market-based, but

I did have about $5,000 in wiggle room in case he made a counteroffer. He responded via email, and it said:

"Thank you for the offer, but I have other offers which are higher. Can you do better?"

In this situation, he was asking me to bid against my initial offer. It's a rookie mistake. First, he replied via email, and I believe discussions about salary should be just that - a verbal discussion (followed-up with an email or another form of writing). I know that sounds old school, but the ability to have difficult conversations with your potential boss illustrates you are not intimidated and that you have the self-confidence to stand up for yourself.

But the more critical issue is that he did not make a counteroffer. He did not say he wanted $15,000, $10,000 or accrued vacation days. He just asked me "to do better." Asking me to "do better" is asking me to bid against myself, which I won't do - and you shouldn't either. Instead, this was my response:

Dear So-and-So,

Glad to hear you are interested in the position. And congratulations on your other offers. This sounds like an exciting time in your professional life! It is our procedure to consult with our HR department to put together a complete package that is both competitive and attractive to potential employees. While we feel the offer was fair, I would certainly consider your counteroffer on your base salary.

We hope you will join us at (company name here) as we have several innovative projects on the horizon which we think would be a great fit with your skills and experience. Feel free to call to discuss.

Sincerely,
Lynn

The result? He asked for an extra $5,000, which is exactly what he got. Both sides walked away happy with this transaction. Yet what if I let my emotions come into the mix and my reaction was (read in a panicky tone for full effect), "Oh no, he wants more money, I better offer him $5,000 so I don't lose him." If I would have taken the bait and negotiated against myself, what do you think would have happened?

He probably would have then made his counteroffer for a higher amount because he would figure I still had more wiggle room since I immediately increased it when he inquired. I shy away from using the word never, but I cannot think of any situation where negotiating against myself has improved my position. So pay attention to the strict formula offer, counteroffer, acceptance or rejection. If you are being asked to vary from this formula, call them out on it and ask them for a counteroffer instead.

Sometimes, you can unintentionally negotiate against yourself. This is where "Jell-O®! language" enters the equation. "Jell-O language" is written or verbal, and it is "wiggly" language which inadvertently gives away your ultimate position or, at the least, information you did not intend to disclose. Here are a few examples of Jell-O language:

1. I can't approve that change. Counter: Who can approve this change?
2. I'm not willing to pay that much now. Counter: When do you think it would be appropriate to spend this type of money?
3. I don't think I can do both. Counter: How about only one?

My favorite, and most annoying example of "wiggly language" came via an email. I was working with a gentleman, who if we were friends would be a frenemy, but since we were colleagues, he would only be described as a "colleugenemy." To say this person didn't value attorney advice on his contracts would be a massive understatement. He didn't care for me, and frankly, I didn't care for him either. But since you have to play nice with others, I tried to make the best of each interaction and learn something in the process. Key word - tried!

We were working on a contract for an important project, significant to both his office as well as his reputation as a client developer. One common provision in construction contracts is called a "limitation of liability." I lovingly referred to that provision as a "LOL" because often it made the client "laugh out loud" when they saw them in their contracts. And not in a good way! In short, a LOL is a risk management tool that is used to limit your total liability for professional negligence to a specific dollar amount. If your LOL was $500,000 and you were professionally negligent, you were only required to pay damages up to $500,000. Even if the result of your negligence exceeded the amount of your LOL. You can see how this provision was not immediately embraced by clients.

I sent our requested changes to the client, and they returned a redlined agreement, indicating what they did and did not accept. Unsurprisingly, they rejected our initial offer of a $500,000 LOL. Since this was a substantial project, our operations leadership team decided they would accept a $2,000,000 LOL given the fees, risk, and relationship with the client, etc. And if we needed to go to $3,000,000, we would. I discussed this with my colleugenemy and thought we were on the same page. I told him that he could offer a $2,000,000 LOL, but if we absolutely had to, we'd be willing to go to $3,000,000. Not that hard, right? Seemed pretty clear from my end. But here is the email that he sent the client:

Dear Client,

Thank you for getting back with us on the changes to the agreement. I think we are pretty close to a resolution. Regarding the LOL, we can do $2 or $3 million. Let me know your thoughts.

Hugs and Kisses,
Colleugenemy

Pop Quiz: Do you think the client requested a LOL in the amount of:
1. $2,000,000
2. $3,000,000

Of course she asked for the $3,000,000! She'd be silly not to ask for $3,000,000. He told her we were willing to go up if she didn't like our first counteroffer. He negotiated against himself by using "Jell-O language." This mistake meant we ended up being on the hook for an extra $1,000,000. That's not chump change. And this could have been avoided while also keeping the door open for them to make a counteroffer. To be fair, I believe that was his intent, but he executed it in an ineffective way. Instead, he could have only offered the $2,000,000 like so:

Dear Client,

Thank you for getting back with us regarding the changes to the agreement. I think we are pretty close to a resolution.

Regarding the LOL, we can increase it to $2,000,000 for this project. If you'd like to discuss these changes, including the LOL, I'd be happy to set up a call or come by your office to answer any questions you may have and get all the details wrapped up. I appreciate you working with us and look forward to moving forward soon.

Sincerely,
Colleugenemy

PS: Our attorney on this is awesome, and I value her counsel on all my projects.

Note the fact that he wrote, "We can increase it to $2,000,000" was a true statement. We had authority to offer that amount. We also had authority to go to $3,000,000, so it would be in our discretion during the negotiation to move up in increments or go straight to $3,000,000. And jumping to our maximum authorized amount would be appropriate if we had information that led us to believe that they were about to walk or that we were somehow in danger of losing the project. No need to dance around and waste time in that situation - get the best terms you can and get to work.

But there were <u>no</u> indications that this was the case with this project. It was the first round of changes, and the client was not expressing frustration with our alterations. Therefore, using "Jell-O language" in this situation only increased our potential liability by $1,000,000. Possibly. Perhaps we would have ended up at $3,000,000 eventually, and the colleugenemy saved us both time. But the point is his poor wording of the counteroffer inadvertently conveyed our final position, and the client benefitted from that knowledge. If someone asked you, "You can buy the car for $5,000, but I'm prepared to sell it for $2,000," which offer would you accept?

Avoiding "Jell-O language" means you should write and speak as concisely as possible. And you need to remain honest. In the above scenario, if the colleaguenemy would have said, "We can do $2,000,000, but that's as high as we're willing to go" that would have been a lie, and I disagree with that tactic. Instead, a simple "We can do $2,000,000" is clear, concise, and honest. But that statement also isn't so firm that it suggests we would not entertain a counteroffer. And that's the balance you want to strike in this type of a counteroffer situation - make your counteroffer known but keep the channels of communications open so you can work through the issue if they object.

Key takeaway - You want to avoid using "Jell-O language" and also listen for it in your counterpart's responses so you can use it to your advantage.

Pro Tip: Don't sacrifice what you want for a "good deal."

While sacrificing is a part of negotiation, don't sacrifice what you want if you don't have a clear reason. Be reasonable in your sacrifices. Every year, I go to an art fair with a group of girlfriends. One year, it fell on my birthday, which also happens to fall on the Kentucky Derby weekend. So of course we wore derby hats to the art fair to celebrate. We had such a great time. We vowed to recreate the fun each May, including the derby hats.

In 2017, I found an artist who had a beautiful photograph of a brightly colored, worn, and battered old door on a stucco building. It had a wide white matte, and I was instantly drawn to it. After doing a couple of laps around all the booths, I decided that print should go home with me. It was $60 unframed. It was the end of the day on the last day of the art fair. When I took the print to the artist to checkout, he made me a deal:

Cool artist dude: "I'll make you the deal of the day if you're interested."
Uncool me: "Oh yeah, what's that?"

Cool artist dude: "I'll give you the large canvas print of that same picture for $150" (it was listed at $300).
Uncool me: "Sounds great. Let's do it."

The problem? I didn't *like* the larger version on canvas. But I was so caught up in getting a "good deal," I simply reacted. I didn't even consider the fact that I preferred the smaller print with the matte to the canvas version. While the smaller version looked like an original, unique piece, the large version looked mass-produced and ordinary. It wasn't the same. I was so set on getting a "good deal" — paying $150 for a $300 print, that I ended up spending twice as much as I wanted and didn't like the result. To add insult to injury, when I got it home, I didn't have a good space to put the print I didn't actually want (insert sad trombone sounds here!).

Sometimes the best thing for the negotiation is to stall and give it some time to breathe. While my preference is to jump in and get things done, every so often you will run into a situation where you should take a breather and disengage. Assuming there is not a hot deadline driving the process, taking a few days to cool down and regain perspective can be a valuable tool. Like relationships, sometimes absence makes the negotiation grow fonder!

The key to managing failure is to keep it in perspective. Try to focus on what you did right instead of what you did wrong. Obviously, you want to learn from your mistakes, but there is a fine line between learning and dwelling. If your internal dialogue is speaking with extremes like "I never," "I always," etc., you are in "dwelling" territory and need to turn it around quickly. The best solution to this is to jump right back in and start a new negotiation. Trust me; you will not get better by thinking about negotiation. You need to be a "doer" to improve. And thankfully, the more you do it, the better you get. Your anxiety about "making the ask" will lessen and may go away completely.

It's rare that I get nervous about negotiating now. But that wasn't always the case. When I first started, I would dread picking up the phone to start the conversation. There would be a least fifteen minutes of mental psych-up time. But repetition made me feel more comfortable and now I pick up the phone without hesitation. When you feel confident in your knowledge, skills, and abilities, your stress level drops, and you can get more done. So instead of using failure as an excuse to stop, use it as fuel to keep going. You will be grateful in the long run.

Conclusion

- The last of The Three R's is to be reasonable. No one likes negotiating with someone who is unreasonable. So, during your preparation stage, you need to ensure you can back up all of your requests with a clear reason.
- Even if you have clear reasons for everything, you can seem unreasonable in your manner. You need to ensure that you control your emotions rather than letting your emotions control you. You can intentionally choose to

show a particular emotion, but only if it is going to help your position. If you let your emotions get out of control, displaying signs of anger, fear, or frustration, you will not be seen as a reasonable negotiator.

- Not only do you want to be reasonable with the other person, you also want to be reasonable with yourself. If you negotiate against yourself, while the other person may appreciate it and take advantage of it, you aren't being reasonable. A negotiation should be offer; counteroffer; then accept the offer, reject the offer, or offer another counteroffer. You should never give another offer or counteroffer until the other party does so first.
- And keep your failures in check. Everyone makes mistakes. It's how you bounce back that really counts.

SECTION V

ADDITIONAL TOOLS AND STRATEGIES

Strategies for Specific Situations

While the Three R's Formula applies to any situation, some specific situations have unique circumstances requiring additional strategies. As I discuss each of these situations, remember everything said in previous sections still applies here.

Situation: Confrontational Negotiation

In my experience, a collaborative and consensus-building style of negotiation is the most effective. Because people help people they like, it's best to start from a positive place. For most situations, I don't recommend a confrontational style to start a negotiation. Of course, the tone of negotiations can sometimes change during the process, so you'll then need to readjust your style. At no point am I asking you to be a doormat. Quite the opposite. If your counterpart starts being a jerk, you need to readjust and assume a more aggressive position.

And when I reference a confrontational style, I'm referring to when people adopt an aggressive approach. This often manifests in harsher tones while speaking, more severe word choice, sharper written communication and sometimes direct threats to end the negotiation. It's the classic "I win, you lose" mindset.

If I don't have advance knowledge that my counterpart will be confrontational, I'm slow to match their style initially because I give people the benefit of the doubt. They may be having a bad day. Their abrasiveness may not be about me or my negotiation at all. Basically, it's a two strikes rule. If it happens a third time, I'll readjust my approach.

This isn't an absolute rule; if their jerkiness is so severe, it may be a one and done scenario that moves me towards a more aggressive style. But I try to not get there too quickly as it is hard to revert from an aggressive style back to consensus building. It can be done, but it's a harder path to navigate.

However, if you gained information during your preparation phase that indicates your interaction will be confrontational, you should be prepared to quickly adjust with a confrontational approach. One way to do this is to mimic your counterparts' style. If they are slow to supply information, you do the same. If they are being short in their communication i.e., no small talk, no niceties, blunt language, etc., do the same (while still remaining professional, of course). Maintain your calm, but speak with a more authoritative tone and with more direct statements. The rule here is basically this: don't be nice to a jerk *and* maintain your professionalism.

Typically, when it's necessary to be adopt a confrontational style, I may try to bring them back to center as the negotiation progresses. I'll test the waters by trying to interact with more of a consensus building tone (in speech or writing). Sometimes, they will drop the confrontational tone and move to a more collaborative position. Their style may be to start all negotiations with an aggressive mindset, but when they see you are not a doormat, they may choose to readjust and focus more on consensus-building.

During an aggressive negotiation, you'll want to keep focused on your walking triggers. You may be tempted to walk over nonessential items because you want to get away from their difficult personality. But if you focus on what you want and what is unacceptable, you'll stay on course and be happy with the results. Keep your emotions in check and keep your focus on the final outcome.

Coping Mechanisms — Managing Conflict

While some negotiations are quick and easily resolved, you will eventually encounter one that brings with it a significant amount of conflict. That conflict could present itself in several ways.

- Timing: It drags out over weeks; months; and possibly, even years.
- Personalities: Your counterpart is a character. And not the good kind! You don't like him/her, and yet you are forced to interact with them to get the project finished.
- Contention: For whatever reason, the negotiation is argumentative or even downright hostile.

When you recognize that conflict has entered the negotiation, the first thing you want to do is say, "Welcome, conflict!" I mean it. It's already here, whether you want it or not. So go ahead and address it. By acknowledging it, you steal a little bit of its power over you. By identifying that there is conflict in the negotiation, you can better deal with it.

Once you roll out the welcome mat, it's time to figure out a way to cope with the conflict. And when I say cope, I'm talking about finding a method you can utilize to help you minimize the adverse effect of the conflict and keep you moving forward. For example, when a negotiation has turned into a snail and is creeping on and on, I tend to get frustrated, which in turn makes me want to express this to my counterpart.

This may or may not be the right thing to do. If they work for a large corporation, which requires excessive hoop-jumping to get approvals, the speed of the negotiation may not be under their control. In this situation, I won't mention anything (unless of course, we are on a specific deadline which needs to be met. That makes the timeline a material issue that needs to be addressed). In these cases, I find it helpful to remind myself that at some point this will be over. It sounds silly, but it gives me comfort knowing I won't have to deal with this negotiation for my entire life. And honestly, when you are in the thick of it, it can feel like that is the case! "Yup, this is my life now. I have to deal with this for the rest of my life. This is what I do. It's how I roll now. Yes, this is it for me." When you start to feel like this, repeat after me "This will end someday. Either we resolve it, or we don't, but it will end at one point." Take a few deep breaths and keep moving forward. There *will* be a resolution at some point.

If the conflict is a personality type, it's also helpful to remind yourself that at one point you will not have to interact with this person again. It will resolve. You will move on. But I find that is only mildly helpful toward managing my emotions toward conflicts with individuals. Instead, I use my favorite filter to determine if I should talk. It's perhaps my favorite piece of advice that I use both professionally and personally:

"If it feels good to say it, don't."

I heard this advice from Major General (retired) Vincent Boles when my husband served with him in the US Army.

It is simple, yet effective. Why? Because when it feels good to say something cutting to someone in the midst of a conflict, you are drawing from an emotional or unprofessional well. For example, imagine a family member starts to criticize you about how you spend your money. The comments are steeped in a passive-aggressive tone and imply you are reckless with your spending. Your blood pressure starts to rise, as you are thinking "What? I have a 401(k), college account, savings, etc. I save *way* more money than you do — Why do you care and how dare you!" Would that feel good to say? You bet. Would it be helpful in resolving the conflict? Probably not.

If it feels good, then you are likely lashing out at the other person and not countering with facts or an opposing view. It's rare for you to "feel" anything when you are speaking with facts or counterarguments (unless it's frustration that your counterpart isn't *listening* to undeniable facts). There is a lack of emotion with facts. So when it would feel good to say something, don't. Like most things, the more you learn to do this, the easier it gets. Much like a muscle, the more you try to *not* say what would make me *feel* good, the stronger and better you will get at it.

Then you'll find yourself thinking things like "Oh my word, I could crush you by bringing up an example where you did the same thing, or worse! But I won't, because it won't be helpful." You feel extremely mature when you start doing this because frankly, it's a mature thing to do. This is exceptionally helpful in personal relationships. Imagine the following example of yourself and your significant other:

Your SO: "Could you put your dirty dishes in the sink if the dishwasher is full? It looks bad and takes up all the counter space?"

You: Think – really? Let's talk for a minute about the books, gear, clothes, shoes, etc. you leave around the house! Instead, you say - "Sure thing. It would be good if we tried to keep things tidier around the whole house."

Trust me. This is a great tool to help keep your emotions in check during a negotiation or any emotional interaction. And it may or may not be the reason I am uncharacteristically quiet during some family get-togethers!

Another tool to managing conflict is to remind yourself that you can always walk away. There are few situations in life where you don't have the choice to walk away. Prison is one of those situations, but let's assume that is not your current (or future) reality. It may be a *bad* idea to walk away, but sometimes, knowing that it is an option, releases the pressure valve in your head and allows you to continue moving forward. And regarding a negotiation, during your preparation phase, you already outlined your walking triggers. So, go back and review those. Remind yourself of your hard stops and your giveables. Sometimes this is enough of a little boost during a contentious interaction to encourage you to stay the course.

Situation: Team Negotiations

There are several situations where you may find yourself in a team negotiation environment — it's not solely you and a counterpart, but you and others on your team. Maybe you and your spouse or partner go to buy a car. Or a house. Or a refrigerator. It doesn't matter what you are negotiating, it matters that you will be working together as a team. Or perhaps you are a salesperson, and you need to team up with someone from operations to cover the technical aspects of a project.

The key to a successful team negotiation is communication, communication, communication. You must be on the same page regarding your prioritized changes, walking points, and financial triggers. Both you and your team have to have a clear understanding of the issues and what you are after in the negotiation. You need to have a connection. And when I say connection, I'm talking a "wink at your dog, and he winks back" sort of connection (dog owners will understand!). Communication on the highest level.

You don't have to be best friends, but have mutually agreed upon objectives and parameters. You can't have an "Ehh, we have to work together so let's get through it" connection. If that is the vibe you have with your partner, it will be much better for you to negotiate by yourself and then contact your partner offline to fill in the necessary gaps.

Thankfully, I have experienced only two team negotiations when my partner turned on me in a panic in a misguided and unnecessary attempt to "save the deal." Once it was with the "colleugenemy" previously mentioned. We had discussed the objectives in advance and had a detailed plan of attack. When we got on the call with the client, he completely abandoned our plan and instead gave in on every provision after only mild questions by the client, which turned the negotiation into a "two against one" dynamic. Obviously, fighting with someone who is supposed to be on your side is a) not productive and b) does not project the most professional dynamic to your counterpart!

The other time was similar. My colleague panicked when the client had detailed questions on our provisions, so he immediately abandoned our plan and agreed with everything the client said because he didn't like conflict. Neither scenario was great and could have been avoided if I had considered the temperament of my teammates more thoroughly. In retrospect, I should have paid more attention to my previous dealings with both these people and should have predicted they would become too emotionally involved when the client was expressing any amount of frustration.

One of my favorite examples comes from the TV show "*My Name is Earl.*" The main character, Earl Hickey, is a special kind of redneck who lives in a motel with his brother, Randy. They own a Chevrolet El Camino, which he is trying to sell to raise money to do a good deed so he is on the right side of Karma. Earl and Randy found themselves on the side of the road when the El Camino ran out of gas, and a guy approached them about the "For Sale" sign in the window. Their team negotiation didn't go so well:

Potential Buyer: "I'll give you $1,800 for it if it runs."
Earl: "It runs, just not right now. It's out of gas."
Potential Buyer: "I'll give you $1,785 for it."
Brother Randy: "Take it, Earl, you know this car isn't worth more than $1,500"
Potential Buyer: "I'll give you $1,500."
Brother Randy: "Take it, Earl, we're desperate!"
Potential Buyer: "$1,200."

Brother Randy: "Hurry Earl! He's lowering his price for no reason!"

End result? They sold their beloved El Camino for $1,200.

I love this illustration for a few reasons. First, it shows the danger of having a team negotiation where both parties are not entirely gelled on the preferred outcome. It also illustrates the downside of negotiating with family!

Good Cop/Bad Cop and the Power of Throwing Someone Under the Bus

One of the most useful elements of a team negotiation is the ability to play "good cop, bad cop." Yes, all those cheesy cop dramas are on to something with this setup. One of the most underestimated tools in negotiation is the ability to strategically throw someone under the bus. Specifically, you want one person to deliver good news, and another person (or department) to cover the bad news.

It sounds counterintuitive, but this little tool allows the negotiator to save face while still communicating the company's position. There are, of course, a few caveats to using this tool. First, you can't overuse it. If you keep saying, "Well, I'd love to let you do that, but so-and-so won't agree," you are undermining your credibility to make a deal. Eventually, your counterpart will want to talk to so-and-so to speak to the person who has all the decision-making capability. So use this tool sparingly.

Second, be sure to tell the person whom you threw under the bus that you used them in this capacity. As an in-house attorney, I often *advised* my internal clients to "blame Legal" when they had to present an unpopular change (even if it was their idea). I asked that they let me know when they did this so when the client called me, I would know they saw me as the "bad guy" and could adjust my responses. It's common courtesy — when using someone as a scapegoat to help the deal, let that person know and have them agree in advance.

Situation: You Aren't Negotiating with the Right Person

Getting to the right person

One of the hardest parts of a negotiation is getting to the right person. There can be multiple layers, it can change at times, and there are egos involved. And sometimes, you know you are not working with the ultimate decision maker, but you must "bloom where you are planted" and do the best you can to start the process.

If you are working with a non-decision maker, meaning a person who has some, but not all, authority to make all the decisions regarding your negotiation, then a "no" is not a "no" until the decision maker gets involved. That's not to say you will talk to them directly. Sometimes the ultimate decision maker is guarded as closely as the Wizard of Oz behind the curtain. But your counterpart will need to talk to them at some point to get their opinion on the matter.

However, figuring out the level of your counterpart's authority can be tricky. You have to establish whether what they are saying is the final word, or if there is someone you can target to escalate the issue. The first way to determine whether they have authority is to listen to their language choice.

Are they using "wiggly" language? For example, "I can't authorize that change" or the equivalent which is "That change exceeds my authority." Indicating that they can't authorize something means there is someone who can — it's simply not within their scope. In that case, you'll want to follow up by asking who *can* authorize the change. Pay attention to their language. Whether it is wiggly or definitive is your first clue to determining their authority.

If their language isn't giving you any clues about their authority level, you need to be direct and ask. You'll want to do this in the politest way possible to protect sensitive egos. Your counterpart may see this as a "vote of no confidence" in their interactions with you. When you damage someone's ego, they won't like you and won't want to help you. In fact, if you don't handle this with care, you risk damaging the entire negotiation.

You don't want to imply you aren't willing to work with that person, but you are merely trying to figure out who can allow the change you are requesting. It's best to ask this question early in the negotiation, if possible, so you appear to be asking for a clarification on scope rather than looking to escalate above their head because you don't like their answer.

Questioning their authority the wrong way can create an air of disrespect that is counterproductive. It's the difference between "Who is the best person to talk to about getting this change approved" versus the loud, suburban mom barking the cringe-inducing phrase "I want to talk to your manager!" Which would you rather hear if you were on the receiving end? The one that implies you don't have authority to make a big decision? Or the one that recognizes it's time to get someone else involved? It's a subtle difference, but an important one. Remember — people help people they like.

Often, issues related to approval authority arise toward the end of the negotiation. Your counterpart will negotiate everything they have power to change but will naturally leave those items that exceed their authority for the end of the discussion. And if you sense you have some issues needing additional feedback from others in the organization, it's best to table those and focus on what your current counterpart *can* approve.

We do this for two reasons. First, it allows you to build a good rapport with your counterpart while you negotiate the terms that are under their control. Second, when you escalate to someone higher, it can be difficult to come back down the food chain. Because there are egos involved, the first person you worked with may get upset that you had to go past them to get what you wanted.

This is by no means an absolute, but it does happen so be aware. Focus on what you can get with whom you are working with, and then take all other issues up with someone else. If you've established yourself as Ready, Relatable, and Reasonable, then it is likely they will give you a positive endorsement when they move you to the decision maker. And that is a valuable asset.

Job Titles

When you meet your counterpart, they will likely have a title that indicates their position. Here's the thing, you can't be intimidated nor impressed by titles. Not even the super fancy titles followed with six different acronyms indicating all their degrees or certifications.

During a negotiation, your authority and influence are what matter. Not your title. I know plenty of people who have impressive titles but don't have authority to tie their own shoes. Banks, I'm looking at you right now! But the flip side is also true. Don't be fooled by someone whose title sounds less than impressive. I've worked with plenty of contract administrators and project managers who have complete authority for the negotiation.

Unless you have first-hand knowledge of a person's authority matrix (perhaps a government official you know can only approve specific changes), you cannot judge a person's level of influence based on their title. President, vice president, director, senior manager, attorney, administrative assistant, paralegal, etc. They don't mean anything unless they have the authority and influence to make your deal. Now, if you are lucky enough to get a person with a big title who has authority, congratulations! Your negotiation will likely go quicker because you don't have to ping-pong back-and-forth to get decisions made. It's a good thing. But don't let titles get in your head.

"LEADERSHIP IS NOT ABOUT TITLE OR A DESTINATION. IT'S ABOUT IMPACT, INFLUENCE, AND INSPIRATION. IMPACT INVOKES GETTING RESULTS, INFLUENCE IS ABOUT SPREADING THE PASSION YOU HAVE FOR YOUR WORK, AND YOU HAVE TO INSPIRE TEAMMATES AND CUSTOMERS."
- ROBIN S. SHARMA, AUTHOR/SPEAKER.

Pro Tip: While we are discussing the topic of assumptions and judgments, pay attention to any gender bias you may have. Having worked primarily in male-dominated fields, I've almost become immune to walking into a meeting with a male subordinate and having the client, vendor, or subcontractor assume the male is the attorney and

I'm a paralegal or assistant. I won't lie, it's annoying. And it makes that person look pretty foolish. If you don't know who is playing what role, ask. There is no harm in asking for clarification, but there is harm in making an incorrect assumption.

Situation: Need to Give an Ultimatum

Once you have made progress with your negotiation, it's possible you will arrive at a sticking point where you cannot find a way to move forward. Obviously, you'll want to try to find a creative and workable solution, but sometimes, you can't get there. That's when you need to consider whether or not you should offer a genuine ultimatum — Give me this, or I walk.

Before giving the "my way or the highway" message, you will want to consider a few things. First, do you want or need to keep this relationship? If the answer is "no," then, by all means, proceed with your final demand. Keep in mind during the days of social media and networking, even if you are proposing a "take it or leave it" scenario, I still advocate doing it professionally. It's a small world, and you still want to have a good reputation. If you can't come to terms with someone, you can't come to terms. It doesn't mean you flip the switch to "they are dead to me now." It's unnecessary and could come back to haunt you later.

Keep in mind that offering an ultimatum does not mean the relationship will end. But it might, so if you can't risk losing that relationship (perhaps it's your biggest client, or they are the industry leader and you know you will need to work with them down the road), then an ultimatum may not be your best bet. Instead, try harder to find a resolution to the issue to continue working together.

> **"DON'T BURN BRIDGES. YOU'LL BE SURPRISED HOW MANY TIMES YOU HAVE TO CROSS THE SAME RIVER."**
> **– H. JACKSON BROWN, JR., AUTHOR.**

And consider if you are ready to end the negotiation. If you are, then proceed. But if you're unsure, then keep trying to find a resolution.

You may be temporarily burned out from the interaction and need a little breathing room to gain perspective. Take a "negotiation vacation" and allow yourself to walk away for a little bit, even if it is just a day of not dealing with that person, contract, topic, or company. You may feel re-energized by taking a brief break.

Finally, if you are presenting an ultimatum to your counterpart, consider throwing someone under the bus as discussed earlier. It can be helpful to have a scapegoat and can serve as a strategic advantage. For example, when I got to the "take it or leave it" point of negotiation while working with engineers, often it was helpful for the engineer to deliver that message.

This did two things. First, it let the engineer be seen as the "good cop" as we covered earlier. "I would agree to this, but Legal wouldn't let me." It was true. And it was likely something their counterpart could resonate with because, as it turns out, almost nobody likes Legal! But it also allows them the opportunity to salvage the relationship because they have someone else to blame. It was out of their control, but they still want to continue to work together on other projects.

All of this was true. I was the one coaching the engineer to blame me because it would help their relationship with the client. I never minded being the bad guy. Now, when they blamed me for something I *didn't* say . . . that was a different story!

Regarding conflict management, you never want to get bullied into a decision by an aggressive negotiator. You know the type: the ones that hound you, they don't take the typical social cues to back off, and they keep going in an attempt to get you to agree to their terms. "Relentless" would be their spirit word.

My favorite example of this is the good ol' mall kiosk workers. Have you ever met more aggressive negotiators? They sharply confront you (trying not to make eye contact is *not* a deterrent to these folks); they don't take the first, second, or third "no" as an answer; and they are more than willing to stalk-walk with you while trying to get you to try their wares.

The key to working with any aggressive negotiator is to first identify them as such. Mentally noting they are a highly-aggressive negotiator is powerful, because it lets you detach from the emotional reaction to aggressiveness. It permits you to react analytically. Second, make sure your politeness doesn't make you do something you don't want to do. Many times, I've seen people agree to terms they didn't want because they got worn down by an aggressive counterpart. Don't do this! You don't owe anyone anything during a negotiation. You can always walk away if you can't get your core terms or your "have to have's." And if you aren't getting what you need from the transaction, it's imperative you walk away. Otherwise, what's the point?

> *I'm walking away*
> *From the troubles in my life*
> *I'm walking away*
> *Oh, to find a better day.*

> *Lyrics from "Walking Away" by Craig David.*

Additional Tools to Help You Succeed

The Three R's are your strongest tools to find success. But additional tools can be used as needed, including competition, post-negotiation analysis and getting everything in writing and becoming a creative negotiator.

<u>Competition</u>

One thing you can use to get better is competition. In my experience, almost everyone has a competitive spirit. And getting better at negotiation is something you can view competitively — either by yourself or others. If you are in a work environment, you can track who gets the best terms, the most deals, or whatever the marker is that your company uses to evaluate success. Car dealerships use cars per month sold. Salespeople often use accounts opened. What is valued at your company? There is always a way to measure success. And when you can measure it, you can make a game of it to motivate yourself and others.

When I managed a corporate Legal Department, I encouraged healthy competition between the lawyers by tracking the amounts of contracts reviewed. When those numbers all became close enough that the winner wasn't a big deal anymore, we tracked the quality of the terms they were getting. How many people secured a limitation of liability? Who was able to close a contract with a new client? Who got better terms with an existing client? With the right group of people, it can keep things fun and exciting.

Some say that I tend to fall on the "hyper-competitive" side of the spectrum. I attribute it to being the youngest child. We tend to want to compete with the older siblings, whether they are aware of it or not. And for the most part, a competitive nature has served me well.

But alas, like most things in life, everything in moderation. Sometimes you can overdo it and turn things into a competition that shouldn't be. For example, my husband and I once both decided to take up meditation. We did the trial version of

"Headspace" which is an application for a guided meditation. The trial has you do ten days of ten minutes of guided meditation. I recommend the program and continue to do it today. However, when we first started, I found myself asking the hubby each morning, "Did you meditate?" If he had and I hadn't done mine, I raced to my office so I wouldn't "lose." I was engaging in competitive meditation without even realizing it! Once I realized what I was doing, I tried to let it go and focus on what was important.

So, if you find yourself getting too wrapped up in a competition, no matter the type, take a breath, step back and recalibrate your intent. And if you are going to meditate, kick its ass and be the best meditator out there. Kidding, kidding!

Post-Negotiation Analysis

You can get bitter, or you can get better, but you can't do both. The two states are mutually exclusive. So, you need to make a conscious choice of how you are going to enhance your strengths, learn from your mistakes and move forward.

In the military, they utilize "After-Action Reports" or "AARs" to provide a retrospective analysis of a mission. After every negotiation, you should do your AAR by asking questions:

1. What went well?
2. What needs improving?
3. What can I do to leverage my strengths in the future and develop my weakest areas?

AARs are my BFFs. Going through this process will improve your learning curve. It forces you to do an unbiased and intentional reflection of the episode, which will provide clarity to how you are doing. It is especially helpful to keep these notes in a dedicated journal. You can review these before your next negotiation, and soon, you will see patterns develop. It's also a fun way to see how far you've come when you go back and see you've corrected areas that were once issues.

If you interacted with someone else, whether it be a friend, spouse, colleague, etc. you'll want to solicit their input as well. And ask them to give you honest feedback - having someone blow smoke will not help you improve. And when you ask for honest feedback, you need to be tough when listening. Don't get defensive, sensitive or emotional. Getting candid feedback is indeed a gift. Run to this step, not away from it. This is where improvement starts to take root.

During your analysis, start asking yourself the following questions:

- Was your preparation sufficient? Did you do enough homework or did something catch you off guard?
- Did you stick to your walking triggers or did you give up something you shouldn't have?
- How were you at managing your emotions? Did you keep them in check or did they get the best of you?
- Were you able to manage the conflict? Or did the whole event get under your skin?
- How was your stress level through the negotiation? Tolerable or stroke-inducing?
- Were you able to get creative in finding a solution?
- Do you feel like you left something "on the table" or are you confident you got the most out of the interaction?
- How did the relationship with your counterpart fare? Is the relationship still intact and on good terms?
- What was the best part of the interaction? What was the worst?
- If you could change one thing about your interaction, what would it be?

- What are the top three things you did well that you want to make sure you take with you into the next negotiation?

If you take the time to answer these questions, your next negotiation will thank you for it. And don't worry that you screwed some things up — you are just beginning. Don't beat yourself up and don't think because it didn't go well once or twice, you can't negotiate. You can do it! You only need more preparation and practice.

You aren't going to look perfect on your first several interactions. You are going to make mistakes. Some of them may be ugly. I've negotiated thousands of times, and I still occasionally have a regret when I'm done with a transaction. Perhaps I feel I gave up a position too soon. Or maybe I let the interaction cause too much stress because I didn't maintain my perspective.

Looking back at your AAR's and seeing improvement provides a source of encouragement. It's the equivalent of having a little cheerleader in your desk drawer who pops up to remind you that you that you can attack anything you want. Most people are quick to forget their strengths and are too eager to focus on their weaknesses. Don't fall into this trap. Just because you have areas to improve now, doesn't mean you won't move those to the "asset" side of the ledger later.

> "TODAY IS A NEW DAY. YOU WILL GET OUT OF IT JUST WHAT YOU PUT INTO IT... IF YOU HAVE MADE MISTAKES, EVEN SERIOUS MISTAKES, THERE IS ALWAYS ANOTHER CHANCE FOR YOU. AND SUPPOSING YOU HAVE TRIED AND FAILED AGAIN AND AGAIN. YOU MAY HAVE A FRESH START ANY MOMENT YOU CHOOSE, FOR THIS THING THAT WE CALL "FAILURE" IS NOT THE FALLING DOWN, BUT THE STAYING DOWN."
> – MARY PICKFORD, SILENT FILM ACTRESS/AUTHOR.

Getting It in Writing

If you have ever interacted with an attorney in any capacity, you have likely heard one of two things: "It depends" or "What do you have in writing?" Using "It depends" is the lawyers' way of presenting two sides of an argument and making you choose. It's the gateway phrase that moves any decision-making capacity from them to you. It's a trade secret and one some lawyers love. But the more important question attorneys love to ask is what is actually in writing. Why? Because that's the only thing you can prove.

We would all love to live in a society where giving your word was sufficient and your side of the story was taken as the Gospel. But it ain't happening. You have to have your agreements in writing. While contracts are the most formal and enforceable way to codify an agreement, you can also utilize email follow-ups to outline the most important terms of your deal.

For instance, after a phone call or in-person negotiation, I like to send a follow-up email outlining all of the agreements. This does two things. First, it gives my counterpart an opportunity to catch any mistakes and add clarification. Second, it creates a paper trail that shows the terms of the deal. This can be valuable later if those terms are questioned. In over twenty years of experience, I've never met anyone who regretted putting their agreed terms in writing. Of course, I've never done criminal law. I imagine people who hired a hit man and have put that in writing regret their decision. But I'm confident, dear reader, that is not you.

Be Creative

If you aren't sure how to go about getting what you want, think what you have to offer in return or how to appeal to the other person. Sometimes this means "thinking outside of the box," as they say.

Story # 1
Once on my drive to work in 2010, I heard on the radio they were giving away tickets to one of my favorite bands, the Turnpike Troubadours. My schedule at the time didn't allow me to listen all day and try to call for free tickets. But, with the concert being sold out, that was my only option.

And I can't express how much I love seeing this band live. If travelling to multiple cities to see them is wrong, I don't want to be right! So instead of getting angry and annoyed with myself that I missed the opportunity to see them because I forgot to buy tickets earlier, I put on my creative "Don't Ask, Don't Get" hat.

I couldn't just call and ask for tickets without offering anything in return. The whole point of them running the promotion is to encourage people to listen all day. What could I do for them that would add value to their position? I thought hard on this issue on my drive to work and came up with what I thought was a long shot.

I've learned over the years that when I feel something has landed in long-shot territory, I remind myself, and continue to remind you, "Don't Ask, Don't Get!" I knew that the radio station was also promoting their effort to raise money for the local pediatric hospital, Children's Mercy Hospital. The programming on the drive home was filled with interviews, testimonials, and educational pieces about the hospital and how they wanted to raise as much money for them as possible. I had donated to Children's Mercy Hospital earlier that year, so I didn't respond to their campaign. But that was my opportunity to put them in a situation to say "yes." So, I emailed the morning host with the following:

> I heard this morning that you have tickets available to see Turnpike Troubadours when they are in town next week. I am a *huge* fan and forgot to order tickets before they sold out, but unfortunately, my schedule doesn't allow me to listen and call in for a chance to win tickets today.
>
> However, I'd like to propose a deal! I know you are currently raising money for Children's Mercy Hospital ("CMH"). Would it be possible

for you to give me two tickets, and I will bring you a check made out to CMH for $150? If not, I completely understand. I want to be clear, this isn't a "Donation check/hostage situation!" I will commit to making the donation either way and will send you a copy of the receipt even if you can't give me tickets since I love the work CMH does in our community too. However, if I could help you raise the station's donation total in exchange for tickets, I'd be happy to do so!

Thanks for considering this idea and have a great day.

Sincerely,

Lynn

Within a few hours, I got an email response indicating they would be happy to make this deal. Keep a few things in mind regarding this transaction:

1. I had absolutely no leverage here. Zip. So instead, I offered something I knew they wanted, even though it was unrelated to what I wanted.
2. I approached them in a positive, upbeat manner.

3. I explained why I couldn't win by calling and also that I'm a huge fan (not someone trolling for free stuff).
4. I recognized they might think it was a bit "blackmaily" to not donate if I didn't get tickets. So, I offered to make the donation regardless.
   a. Keep in mind here the goal was to *get* the tickets. Not get a *deal* on the tickets. If I had my act together and purchased them in advance, I would have paid around $50 or less.
5. I recognize that some may think this is unfair to others who were trying to call in and win. I'm not sure how many tickets they had to give away. But I don't regret offering them a creative solution that benefitted us both. If I didn't have the money to donate (and at many times during my career, I did not), I would have offered something else. Perhaps volunteering at their next charitable event.

The point here is that it's not about the money or having leverage. It's about thinking about a win-win solution and having the guts to ask in a likable and reasonable way. This is how you get a high success rate.

Story #2

My son, Jack, had no hair his first year. A little peach fuzz, but basically a cue ball for the first ten – fourteen months. When he finally grew hair, it was white-blonde and started to curl at the ends. When he turned two, I saw an adorable head of curly hair. My husband saw a mullet.

To be fair, my husband was right. It was definitely entering mullet territory when Jack's hair was longer and curling in the back (the true definition of "business in front and party in the back"). My husband mentioned that it was probably time for his first haircut. For some irrational reason, the idea of getting his hair cut terrified me. I thought his childhood would somehow end once we cut the curls! It wasn't logical. It was bonkers. I can admit that now. But instead of overcoming my neurosis, I did what I do best — I negotiated!

It was early October, so I quickly brainstormed a Halloween costume that would justify Jack having a mullet for a few extra weeks. I knew he would have to *eventually* get a haircut. I wasn't that removed from reality. But I figured if I could incorporate the mullet into a costume, I could buy myself a few extra weeks with the cute curls. Sure enough, I negotiated with my husband to keep the mullet for a few extra weeks so Jack could be Benjamin Franklin for Halloween. It was epic!

My favorite part was when we went to the park with neighborhood kids and they were all running around in superhero outfits, someone would ask Jack what he was, and he would do his best to say "Benjamin Franklin" in his two-year-old voice. I always knew that my ability to choose Halloween costumes for him had a short shelf life. And I'm grateful I was able to negotiate my child's mullet into an epic Halloween costume. No regrets.

> "THE TRUE SIGN OF INTELLIGENCE IS NOT KNOWLEDGE BUT IMAGINATION."
> – ALBERT EINSTEIN, THEORETICAL PHYSICIST.

Conclusion

- Be prepared and adjust when you run into a counterpart who uses a confrontational style. Do not be a doormat!
- Outline the coping mechanisms you will use to help manage conflict. Including the important "If it feels good to say it, don't" rule.
- Evaluate your teammate carefully whenever you are engaged with team negotiations. You must both be on the same page. And remember that good cop/bad cop is an effective strategy when used appropriately.
- Learn how to get to the right person. And be careful when you chose to issue an ultimatum.
- Use competition and post-negotiation analysis to help you continuously improve.
- And don't forget two of my favorite rules: 1) Be creative, 2) Get it in writing!

SECTION VI

GETTING STARTED

How to Start

You already know that the best way to improve a new skill is to practice. But where do you start practicing with negotiation? You could start with negotiating your salary and benefits with your next job offer, but you should exercise this muscle with less important items to build up both your skill set and your confidence. You could buy a new car or appliance to practice, but you should start somewhere smaller to have less at stake and give you an opportunity to practice "Making the Ask" and getting some small wins under your belt, which helps build your confidence.

So instead, look for opportunities to make "easy asks." These are somewhat passive questions, prompts really, that get you in the habit of "Making the Ask." Here are some examples:

Would it be possible if we . . .?
Would you consider doing . . .?
You know what I'd love to do/have?
What would you say to doing X instead of Y?
Do you think you could help me by...?
What if we did . . .?
Is there any way we can . . .?

Using "we" in this way is intentional. It implies a connection or partnership with your counterpart. It's subtle but effective. Again, these are passive questions, intended for you to practice asking the question to start a negotiation. It's the old Wayne Gretzky premise "You miss 100% of the shots you don't take." If you can't ask the question to start a negotiation, then you aren't going to have an opportunity to practice your negotiation skills!

You'll be surprised how comfortable you become starting a negotiation once you practice "Making the Ask." It's because engaging in small-stakes negotiations begins to take the fear out of the process. You start to realize the worst thing they can do is say "no." And many times, they say "yes," or at least some version of "yes." And when you are engaging The 3 R's Formula of being Ready, Relatable and Reasonable, you get positive responses. And when you get positive responses, you gain confidence. And as you know, confidence in a negotiation is your invisible secret weapon.

When you are confident in your negotiation skills and execution, you exude strength and calmness that the other side will notice. And that is worth the practice! Imagine going into a negotiation of any type (salary, car, home or contract) and feeling comfortable that you not only know what you are doing, but that you know you are going to be getting more for yourself because you are asking for what you want, counter-offering to get there and will not compromise on your core issues. That's a powerful feeling, right? And one worth pursuing.

Once you are comfortable using these passive prompts to get a negotiation started, it's time to start tightening up your language. It's not an enormous difference, but it is more assertive than the first version. And if you are practicing your negotiation skills in your professional life, go ahead and jump straight to the more assertive language since it has a more professional tone (depending, of course, on your industry). Consider the following:

Passive prompt	**More Assertive language**
Would it be possible if we…	I'd like to discuss doing/changing/adding, etc.…
Would you consider doing . . . ?	Can we agree to . . . ?
You know what I'd love to do/have?	I'd like to . . .
What would you say to doing X instead of Y?	I'd like to make the following change…

When at work, it helps to keep a sticky note with these starters as a quick reference. It will serve as a visual prompt to remind you to "Make the Ask."

Venues to Practice

Finding environments to practice negotiation is essential. Here are a few low-stress, low-pressure environments to get started:

1. Garage sales. A classic "haggling" environment. It is well known that negotiating prices at a garage sale is an

acceptable practice. So you don't have the "Should I even be asking?" cloud hanging over your head. Plus, you aren't haggling over high-dollar items or the "absolutely can't live without" level of attachment.

Some introductory language to get you started:

"I'd love to take this piece home, but it's too much for me right now. Is there any wiggle room on the price?"

-Or-

"This piece is amazing — I bet you loved having it! Is there any way we could bring the price down? I'd love to enjoy it in my home!"

2. Online purchases. The chat function can be a comfortable "entry level" place to practice negotiation. Any time you are making a purchase and see that the company has "promo code" section during checkout, you may have an opportunity to negotiate.

Knowing that they have promotional codes available, you can always search Google for a code, but why not just ask? See if they have a chat function. If there is, just ask them if there is a discount code available for you to use. You'll be surprised at how often you will get a 10% or 25% discount just by asking. No chat function? Email them with the same question. Talk about a low-stakes, low-pressure environment! But the important part is that you are teaching yourself to "Make the Ask."

I was ordering a product from a new company recently and had to email them a question about the product. They responded to my question promptly. Right before I made my purchase, I saw the "promo code" box, and I had a "Don't Ask, Don't Get" moment. I emailed them again and asked if they had a promo code for a first-time buyer (there wasn't anything on Google). They sent me a code for 50% off my first order! Not only was I excited to save money, but they also made me a loyal customer. A true win-win.

3. Furniture/appliance stores. Styles change, and they work in a high-turnover industry. Do your research. Point out nicks and scratches if you are interested in the floor model. Be sure to know details about their product. And always ask for free delivery!

4. Cable/phone bills. Because it's cheaper to keep an old client than to recruit a new one, they are quick to find a new deal to convince you to stay. Annoying, but true. So don't be afraid to threaten to leave - they can't actually *make* you leave if you change your mind and decide to stay. But you may get a better deal just by asking

5. Credit card companies. Similar to the cable company, many credit card companies will work with you to either reduce your interest rate (assuming you have a good repayment history and credit score — if either one of these are poor, you are looking at an uphill battle). Or they can move you to a card that has more incentives if you ask.

Again, this is a situation where there is no downside to calling them and seeing what you can get, as they won't dump you for just asking! Push them with polite but pointed questions if you aren't getting an immediate win. "What programs are available to me?" "What else can you offer me as an incentive to keep my business with you?" "When am I eligible for an incentive upgrade?" Perhaps you'd like a higher limit on the card — go ahead and "Make the Ask." This is a classic "Don't Ask, Don't Get" scenario.

Timing

> "THE SCARIEST MOMENT IS ALWAYS BEFORE YOU START. AFTER THAT, THINGS CAN ONLY GET BETTER."
> – STEPHEN KING, AUTHOR.

The first thing to consider when you start a negotiation is timing. When is the best time to negotiate? Typically, the best time is *before* you deliver any benefits of the deal. For example, if you are providing a professional service, you need to negotiate the terms of the agreement before you provide the services.

But sometimes you need to get started before you negotiate the terms of the deal. When I first began reviewing contracts in the construction industry, I was on the phone with one of my engineers discussing the changes I made to the client's contract. He was polite and listened to all my points. Then he said, "Okay, but you do realize we've already done the work, and we've already provided our report, right?" What?! As soon as we were done with the call, I ran down the hall and told my boss. I was sure this was a monumental failure on the engineers' part and this was a complete fluke.

My boss's response? "Welcome to the construction industry!" I was shocked. But I soon learned that sometimes in that industry, weather and timing are more important than contract terms. And if you have an existing relationship with your client, it's sometimes acceptable to move forward initially without anything in writing. This blew my legal mind! But that is the state of the industry. Over the past fifteen years, negotiating after the work begins has undoubtedly decreased (blame the darn lawyers!). But sometimes, you have to roll with the punches and make the best out of your situation.

Quirky industries aside, most of the time you can negotiate the terms of your transaction before goods or services are exchanged. And that's how you want it. If you already have "skin in the game," your options may be limited. For example, it's harder to say you will walk if you've already spent time or money on the project. The opposite party knows you don't want to leave money on the table. Your power to delay or stall in order to create more time to get things done is also reduced because you are already doing the work.

Managing Your First "No"

At some point, sometimes sooner rather than later, you are going to get your first "no." It's coming, so don't be surprised. But don't get discouraged. Instead, take the Jocko Willink approach. Jocko is a former U.S. Navy Seal, podcaster, New York Times bestselling author, and all-around badass. He has a great philosophy on conflict or rejection — you need to respond to adversity with one word: "Good."

Wait, you're probably thinking, "I thought the whole goal of this book was to make me a better negotiator. Why would I say "good" when I hear my first rejection?" Two reasons. First, it's going to happen at some point so you might as well welcome it when it does. Second, responding with "good" means you change your mentality from one of defeat to one of creatively facing a challenge. Saying "good" means you are going to get creative and figure out how to change that "no" to a "yes."

Once you've established your "good" mindset after hearing a "no," you need to define the *why* behind the "no." What is the basis for their reason to say "no"? Perhaps they physically cannot accommodate your request. Is there something they could do instead that is *close* to what you are asking? Or if it exceeds their authority as discussed above, then who can approve the change?

This is where you combine all your skills to determine the *why* behind their "no." Look to their nonverbals. Are they shifting around when they answer? If so, they may not want to go through the hassle of making the change. If that's the case, ask them what they could do instead of giving you what you requested. Is there a junior varsity version of your varsity level request that you would find acceptable? If you are pitching a professional service and hear a "no," is it "no" right now or "no" forever? Ask your counterpart: "What would it take to make this a "yes"? Perhaps it's a "no" for this project because they are using a new vendor, but they will consider you for future work.

The key is to keep drilling down with specific questions until you can determine the root reason why the answer was "no." This is helpful information not only for the remainder of the negotiation, because you can adjust your reasoning and your changes. But it also helps with future dealings since you will know their sticky issues and what they are not willing to compromise. Thus, you don't waste time asking for things you *know* will be rejected. And your counterpart will take note that you readjusted your tactics to reflect their position, which may make you more likable. And being likable makes it more probable they will do you a favor in the future.

> **DON'T LET WHAT YOU DON'T KNOW SCARE YOU, BECAUSE IT CAN BECOME YOUR GREATEST ASSET. AND IF YOU DO THINGS WITHOUT KNOWING HOW THEY HAVE ALWAYS BEEN DONE, YOU'RE GUARANTEED TO DO THEM DIFFERENTLY.**
> **– SARA BLAKELY, FOUNDER OF SPANX.**

Sara Blakely, founder of Spanx and America's first self-made female billionaire, knows the benefit of not stopping with the first "no" and the importance of getting to a decision maker. When she had perfected her Spanx undergarment, she called the closest Nieman-Marcus and asked if they wanted to buy it. The person on the opposite end of the phone laughed and replied, "Honey, we have a buyer in Dallas that does all that stuff." Her response? "Okay, can I have that number?" Talk about a "Don't Ask, Don't Get" moment!

She then called the buyer in Texas and offered to fly to Dallas if she would give Sara ten minutes of her time. During her uber-short presentation, she could see by watching the buyer's nonverbals that she was losing her. So she asked the buyer to follow her into the ladies room so Sara could show her the before and after of using Spanx on her own rear-end.

The result? She landed Spanx in seven stores and changed the trajectory of her life and women's rear-ends around the world. On behalf of all the women who now rely on Spanx as an integral part of our wardrobe, a heartfelt "thank you" to Sara Blakely for asking, and getting, what she wanted and not stopping at her first "no."

Conclusion

- Start small, using the prompts for some "easy asks." As with all things, it takes practice, so find venues where you can practice the art of negotiation.
- Be prepared to get your first "no." When you do, say "good" and learn from it. Find out the reason for their "no" and if you can turn that "no" into a "yes."
- Make sure that you are Ready, Relatable, and Reasonable as you practice. If you need a quick refresher on each of The Three R's, read the conclusion in each of the sections.

- Practice doesn't necessarily make perfect, but practice will increase your odds. So don't just practice and expect results. Instead, take action and apply the principles, tools, and strategies contained in this book, and you will see continued improvement.

SECTION VII

NOW IT'S YOUR TURN!

Congratulations! You now know how to crush your fears, develop your negotiation muscle and gain power in the workplace.

I truly believe that everyone can be a great negotiator. This is not a skill that is limited to those "born with it" or those who've been mentored for years. By preparing and practicing the Three R's, you will continue to increase your confidence in all your negotiations, both personally and professionally.

By studying the concepts in *Negotiate It!,* you've learned how to "Make the Ask." Putting the Three R's into practice allows you to develop confidence, learn how to defend your position, when to anticipate pushback and how to complete your negotiations strategically and efficiently. You have now developed the "Don't Ask, Don't Get" mindset.

Once you have that valuable mindset, you'll see opportunities to negotiate all around you. So go forth and negotiate!

Contact me with your wins, challenges and lessons learned.

Email me at: Lynn@lynnpriceconsulting.com

        Happy Negotiating!

ABOUT THE AUTHOR

E. Lynn Price is a licensed attorney with over twenty years of experience in finding innovative legal, business, and human resources solutions for businesses and business professionals. She is a highly ranked presenter and trainer on negotiation, human resources, and a variety of legal topics.

Lynn has worked for a national engineering firm, a major telecommunications company, a boutique mergers & acquisition firm, and even had a short stint with an award-winning advertising firm. As the leader of a corporate Legal Department of a national company, her team was awarded the "top corporate service department" several times by the company's business unit leaders for offering timely and creative legal services in a high-paced environment. She did this by adopting a *"Be a Resource, Not a Roadblock"* philosophy for herself and her department.

In 2014, Lynn was designated a "40 Under 40" by Ingram's Business Magazine in Kansas City. She is a proud alumnae of Kansas City's Centurion program, a highly-selective program of the Greater Kansas City Chamber of Commerce which educates and develops emerging leaders.

Lynn currently lives near the beautiful Boston Mountains in Fayetteville, Arkansas, which is routinely listed in the top five most livable cities by US News & World Reports.

She's married to a man who smiles and winks at her when he tells others that he "married better than she did." She has a son who is smart and funny and, as a pre-teen, still seems to like her. Lynn has two dogs, Gunner and Scout, who spend most of their days sleeping, looking at her adoringly, occasionally digging up flower beds and jumping on guests.

To contact Lynn for personalized training seminars, speaking engagements or human resource consulting, please go to www.lynnpriceconsulting.com for more information.

www.ingramcontent.com/pod-product-compliance
Lightning Source LLC
Chambersburg PA
CBHW032034290426
44110CB00012B/797